Backing W

Bernice Cohen is the country's best-known finance advisor and is the author of the bestselling books, *The Armchair Investor*, *The Money Maze* and *Financial Freedom*. She presented the popular Channel 4 TV series *Mrs Cohen's Money* and is often seen on financial TV programmes and at investment conferences.

Previous books by the author

The Cultural Science of Man (3 volumes)
The Edge of Chaos
The Armchair Investor
The Money Maze
Financial Freedom
Treasury of Investment Wisdom
The Wealthy Investor

Backing Winners

Bernice Cohen

Lieber Christoph,

Further help for you to make your fortune!

Happy 22nd Birthday.

Much love

Kathrin

XXX

P
PROFILE BOOKS

2002

If you would like to receive a free email newsletter that contains information and features about current and future business books published by Profile Books, please contact us through:
business@profilebooks.co.uk

First published in Great Britain in 2002 by
Profile Books Ltd
58A Hatton Garden
London EC1N 8LX
www.profilebooks.co.uk

1 3 5 7 9 10 8 6 4 2

Typeset in Lapidary 333 by MacGuru
info@macguru.org.uk

Printed and bound in Great Britain by
Clays, Bungay, Suffolk

A CIP catalogue record for this book is available from the British Library.

ISBN 1 86197 446 9

WARNING

Stock market investments (including gifts and loan stocks), unit trusts, investment trusts, insurance products, property and alternative investments, can go down as well as up. The income from most securities can also go down as well as up. When you seek advice, also ask about marketability. The shares, gifts, loans, stocks, investment trusts and unit trusts referred to in the text of this book are for illustrative purposes only and are not an invitation to deal in them. This book was originally written in the summer and autumn of 2001. But market conditions change. Neither the publisher nor the author accept any legal responsibility for the contents of the work, which is not a substitute for detailed professional advice. Readers should conduct their own investment activity through an appropriately authorised person.

Contents

To dear Ildi, Tricia and Dianna
With much love

Preface

If you aren't willing to own a share for ten years,
then don't own it for ten minutes
Warren Buffett, investment guru

Do you remember what you were doing in November 1989 when the Berlin Wall was demolished?

Major moments in history become etched into our collective memories. The day in November 1963 when President Kennedy was assassinated, or 11 September 2001, when Islamic terrorists destroyed the twin towers of the World Trade Center are similar moments when our familiar world faced a dramatic turning point.

Sometimes, personal turning points can be equally significant within the small sphere of family, friends and colleagues; November 1989 was just such a turning point for me, although it was years before I recognised it as such.

In 1989 I was drowning in debt following the collapse of a self-publishing venture. Yet within four years I was describing my investment activities in a column for the *Mail on Sunday*, from which came the offer to make two television series of *Mrs Cohen's Money* for Channel 4 on investing and personal finance. Orion published my first investment book, *The Armchair Investor*, which explained the system I developed to rebuild the family finances by investing in the stock market. Other books on personal finance and investment have followed.

Despite numerous mistakes and false trails en route, one decade has totally transformed our financial situation. From deep and troublesome debt to financial security in one busy drive. The large new mortgage we acquired in 1990 when we moved to a smaller house was completely repaid after nine years, leaving us debt-free. And although my original aim had simply been to get out of debt and rebuild our savings ready for retirement, my investment choices allowed us to build a substantial portfolio of shares, mainly held in two tax-friendly Personal Equity Plans (Peps) where no capital gains tax applies.

How was this exciting transformation achieved? Initially, the most important issue was to face up to the problem of a difficult debt-driven existence that showed no signs of easy resolution. Not a happy prospect for a couple in their early fifties.

Recognising the problem was the central piece in the jigsaw of rebuilding the family fortunes. Moving to a smaller house enabled us to repay the assorted outstanding jumble of credit card and overdraft debts, leaving us with one big mortgage but giving me a modest lump sum with which I planned to begin investing. While this sounds like a reckless gamble just ten years before retirement age, I had watched my father making money by investing in shares in the period between 1968 and 1972. His successes pointed me in that direction.

What I needed was a disciplined approach and a definite goal. Setting myself a suitable goal was simple: get out of debt and rebuild the family's savings ready for a debt-free retirement. Organising the disciplined approach was far more taxing. In 1990, when I began there were very few investment books on the UK stock market and even fewer bookshops housing the US-based books that were available. Trial and error was the only path I could follow but over the past decade I have met hundreds of people at money shows and conferences or during the filming of *Mrs Cohen's Money* who have constantly reminded me of the difficulties people face when trying to turn around a poor financial situation.

Although there are now several books on different ways to

proceed, including those I have written, new ideas that might appeal to novices or investors seeking a fresh approach are always welcome. *The Armchair Investor* was an account of the system I use myself to spot companies that will give an investor handsome returns in due course: *The Wealthy Investor* was designed to guide investors as they move through a series of stages to improve their investment expertise without taking too many risks along the way.

Investing to improve your financial circumstances needs a personal angle, probably unique to each individual, but I know from meeting different people that many want a workable system that does not involve an inordinate amount of time and effort. Recent events have highlighted the poor performance records of professional fund managers and the risks attached to suitable pension plans. These difficulties heighten the need for investors to steer a sensible path through the endless detours and arrive at an exciting destination – a healthy portfolio of shares that can serve as a nest egg to pay for school fees, a foreign holiday home or just a fat cushion to provide cash through the long years of retirement most of us can look forward to. This is the niche that *Backing Winners* will fill, especially for investors who want to make substantial returns from the stock market but are looking for a 'keep-it-simple' approach.

Activity in the markets seems to reach an ever-more hectic pace, while the introduction of new technology is accelerating so rapidly that those companies who fail to innovate can quickly become outdated. As we have repeatedly seen with large reputable companies like BT and Marks & Spencer, no business, however long established, can afford to become complacent. By the time *Backing Winners* is published the performance of some of the companies featured may have changed. The ideas and information presented should be treated as a blueprint, a hands-on guide of what to do and how to do it. The system is versatile and must remain flexible; it does not create a recipe to be slavishly followed. Use the Ten-point Action Plan to search for and buy winning companies you can support over the long term while rejecting the losers that may damage your goals of building a bountiful nest egg.

The best way to make your dreams come true is to wake up

Yurok Indian saying

1 The Ten-point Action Plan

An investor only has to do a small number of things right and avoid making major mistakes to be outstandingly successful

Warren Buffett, investment guru

Thousands of investors dream of making huge profits from the stock market; this is the Holy Grail for investment success. Sadly, most of us ruin our chances by selling profitable shares too soon while holding losers too long. Most investors, myself included, succumb to this losing tactic at times. Avoid repeating it in future by using a focused regime. *Backing Winners* is a blueprint to turn pipedreams of owning big winners into a successful strategy by pursuing the *tens* – follow the *Ten*-point Action Plan, create a *Ten*-bagger Portfolio (of companies that grow *ten*fold while you hold them) to include *ten* exciting prospects and run it for *ten* years to reap the fullest benefits. Your target is to turn *ten* thousand pounds into £100,000 after *ten* years. That prepares you for the mega-leap – to turn £100,000 into £1 million, by continuing the strategy for another *ten* years. By pursuing your winning formula for a second decade, £100,000 could become £1,000,000 as you apply the expertise accumulated during the first *ten* years, to enhance further success. Even if you never reach the magic £1 million, you will be amazed at how dramatically your wealth can grow, to pay off your mortgage or other major debts or travel the world, by following this Ten-point Action Plan.

'The next Microsoft?'

Most investors fantasise about finding 'the next Microsoft' while it is still a small company. Last year my secretary Pat revealed how she once glimpsed this elusive prize. Some years earlier a friend talked glowingly about a recent investment, urging Pat to copy her. Although tempted, Pat was deterred by the cumbersome procedure of opening an online account. Enthusiasm wilted and she never bought those shares but within a few years she realised what she had missed as the company was AOL (America Online), the Internet service provider. Her wistful expression reflected huge regret for that lost opportunity.

Sadly, pinning down 'the next Microsoft' is hard. Staying with your choice while it grows to fulfil its promise is even harder. The strategy involves risk as investing in young start-ups entails a rocky ride. Managing growth is among the most hazardous feats small firms face. Even backing major companies pursuing fast growth can prove disappointing. Thousands of firms will fail utterly before they are anywhere near approaching Microsoft's soaring success; when a company fails, shareholders' lose their whole investment. It can take years before true stars repay your early allegiance and along the route you must keep faith if you are to reap the full rewards. That is perhaps the greatest test of commitment. However, success is within anyone's reach by following the Ten-point Action Plan described in *Backing Winners.*

Search for 'Ten-baggers'

Peter Lynch, the fabled American fund manager introduced an inspiring idea – ten-bagger companies, whose shares grow your wealth ten times over while you own them. The term 'ten-baggers' came from American baseball, but as a target for success with stock market investments, nothing could be more apt. Shares in Orange, the mobile telecoms company, illustrate the possibilities. Orange passed through several hands during 1999 and 2000, being first taken over by Mannesmann of Germany, which was itself bought by Vodafone, before being sold on again to France Telecom and then partially refloated on the French and UK stock markets in 2000. However, from flotation in 1996, when the shares traded at around 200p, to the Mannesmann takeover in winter 1999, the share price rose to over 2,000p (£20). For ten-bagger returns, simply add a nought: a share bought at 100p must rise to 1,000p (£10). It seems beyond reach but the 1990s produced numerous examples: Perpetual and Royal Bank of Scotland in addition to Orange. Look at how an investment of £1,000 in 1990 into each of three fast-growing small companies had risen by June 2001:

Sage Group returned around £25,000, a growth of 2,400 per cent
Vodafone returned around £13,500, a growth of 1,250 per cent
Logica returned around £18,000 or 1,700 per cent

If you can dream it, you can do it
Walt Disney, feature-length cartoon film pioneer and inventor of Mickey Mouse

Follow simple guidelines

As very few UK companies turn out to be candidates for massive growth, the search for ten-baggers can be like chasing rainbows. A hit-and-miss attack is futile: to unlock fully the potential of the ten-bagger idea you need a focused strategy.

Like most skilled tasks, backing winners looks easier in hindsight. Success stems from following a few simple guidelines, as will be explained in later chapters: first, aim to maximise the possibilities of backing winners; second, reduce the risk of backing losers; third, adopt a low risk profile by spreading your funds among several companies and investments and, finally, track the progress of your ten-bagger portfolio to stay on target.

The layout of *Backing Winners* is designed to take you through all the stages of a focused, winning strategy. In this chapter we look at the important big picture, and describe the Ten-point Action Plan, the winning formula to follow. Establishing the big picture is a vital step that sets the scene for everything else. Chapter 2 explores the profile of ten-bagger companies, so we can recognise them while they are young and relatively unknown. Chapter 3 compiles all the warning lessons on recognising loser profiles. Chapter 4 examines the ten most common mistakes investors make so you can avoid them and tilt the odds more firmly towards success.

Design your portfolio to spread risk and minimise the financial impact of failures, a topic covered in Chapter 5. Knowing what you want to achieve – a tenfold return in ten years – is fine, as long as you know how to turn goals into reality. Knowing where to find future ten-baggers forms the basis of Chapter 6 while Chapter 7 looks at the final selection of candidates. By paying attention to calculating buy prices and following the market action, discussed in Chapter 8, you again enhance the possibilities of being right more often than you are wrong. Chapter 9 deals with tracking the progress of the ten-bagger portfolio. Chapter 10 puts the whole Ten-point Action Plan into context to chart success.

The Ten-point Action Plan

Charlie Munger, the business partner of legendary investor Warren Buffett, offered this sound advice, 'You do better to make a few large bets and sit back and wait ... There are huge mathematical advantages to doing nothing.'

Recently my attitude towards my shareholdings has changed as I now regard myself as a part-owner in the companies where I hold shares. Thinking like an owner colours your whole investment philosophy. I heartily recommend every investor try this. I now see that overtrading is a no-win game because too frequent buying and selling means turning over the shares in the portfolio before they have fulfilled their long-term potential. Perhaps most serious investors arrive at this conclusion eventually, but some reach this great milestone earlier than others. I did make money when I was overtrading, but I think the whole philosophy of frequent trading misses the big plot. Unless you are seeking an adrenalin rush, overtrading is a losing strategy. It is counterproductive for building long-term wealth. All the evidence supports this unwelcome conclusion.

Just a few key factors are essential for achieving long-term targets for wealth creation. They are listed here and covered in later chapters in detail as together they form the main elements of the Ten-point Action Plan. Follow the basic guidelines of the Ten-point Action Plan and you are well on your way to hitting whatever investment targets you set:

The Ten-point Action Plan

1. Have a winning vision. Set financial targets for your wealth-creating efforts. Adopt a proven system for backing winners, such as my FASTER GAINS formula and the Ten-point Action Plan covered in later chapters
2. Maximise the possibilities of backing winners by identifying the winners' profile
3. Learn to sell losers early, by identifying the recurring pattern for the losers' profile
4. Tilt the odds more firmly towards success by avoiding the ten most common mistakes investors make
5. Design a low-risk balanced portfolio of wealth-creating assets for your Total Wealth Package and learn where to find essential information on suitable ten-bagger companies

6 Treasure hunt for strong ten-bagger prospects, compiling a preliminary short-list
7 Reduce your list to ten favourite candidates
8 Devise a sensible buy plan to avoid overpaying and spot good buying opportunities
9 Keep tracking your chosen companies within your ten-bagger portfolio
10 Make investing a hobby for life

Since the industrial revolution started, every century has had faster growth than the previous one, and our own will be no different

Michael Mandel, economics editor of *Business Week*

The past is history

One of my first purchases as a novice investor in the summer of 1990 proved a harrowing but ultimately useful experience. On advice I read in a newsletter plus a newly launched investment magazine, both featuring Polly Peck as a 'buy', I bought shares in that company. It had been the fastest growing company in the 1980s decade. Polly Peck was a European agricultural produce supplier that grew from a minnow to enter the prestigious FTSE 100 in 1990 when it was valued at £2 billion, a meteoric rise. Imagine my consternation when within three months I discovered in the *Sunday Times* that it was under investigation for fraud. Horrified by the possibility of suffering a large loss, I sold my shares as the market opened on the following Monday morning and lost 25 per cent of my investment. But continuing rumours about the company sent its shares spiralling lower. As I followed the unfolding drama, I realised that alert small investors can be successful because press coverage showed that several fund managers held their Polly Peck shares until they were suspended. More than a decade later the shares have never yet been relisted, meaning that those fund managers had to write off their complete investment in the company. Judged against their performance my loss of 25 per cent looked modest. Moreover, Barclays Bank, one of the UK's four major high street banks, had lent the Polly Peck chief executive, Asil Nadir, around £4 million so he could buy more shares as a sign of confidence in the company's future. All these professionals had misjudged the firm, standing passively by until the final collapse robbed them of their chance to act. Ordinary shareholders, including fund managers buying shares on behalf of clients to their funds, rank right at the bottom of the creditors' list for payouts in a bankruptcy. When accountants are finally called in to sort out the mess, ordinary shareholders may suffer a total loss, as in the Polly Peck saga.

Assessing this behaviour by professionally managed funds quickly convinced me that paying greater interest to the performance of my wealth-creating targets could bring handsome returns and soon led me to taking greater control over my investments. In retrospect, I was lucky to begin investing at a time of high returns. We can see by the large numbers of valuable companies that grew during the past decade that the 1990s was a superb time for ten-bagger hunters. I would have been less successful if the 1990s had been a poorer investment climate and unnumbered mistakes en route would have reduced my returns.

In July 2001 stock market historian David Schwartz cautioned in the *Financial Times* that long-term investing is less profitable than widely believed as most twenty-five year periods, the typical time investors leave their capital at risk in the markets, had produced meagre profits. He thought the last twenty-six years were exceptional: an investment of £150 in December 1974 in the FT Ordinary index, which tracks thirty major UK companies, had risen by August 2001 to over £3,000 without adding reinvested dividends.

Other benchmark indices endorse the market's excellent performance over two decades. In 1980 the FTSE All-Share benchmark index of around 750 UK listed companies stood at 230 and ended the millennium at 3,242, again ignoring the benefits of dividends reinvested. As the lists for the top 350 companies are changed every three months to exclude the worst fallers and replace them with new risers, the FTSE All-Share index is perhaps the most representative benchmark that tracks the UK stock market performance. In fact, by eliminating the losers it is actually backing winners! Looking further back, the FTSE All-Share stood at 100 in April 1962, implying that prices more than doubled from 1962 to 1980. In short, the evidence confirms that anyone who had invested money in the stock market for any ten-year period over the past twenty-five years would have done well and the chances of making a positive return were greatest the longer the money stayed in the market.

The performance of technology-based investments was equally impressive. Figures from Autif (Association of Unit and Investment Trusts) show an investor who saved £50 per month in one of the few technology funds available in 1986 would have built a fund worth around £31,687 by August 2001 even after a year of collapsing technology share prices. This compared with £19,815 for a fifteen-year, £50-a-month saver in an average UK companies fund.

Back to the future

Well, the past, as they say, is history. But even if David Schwartz is right about future returns, profits can be improved many times over by following a successful system to back winners and sell losers. A good stock picking system really is worth its weight in gold. There is convincing evidence for the value of good stock picking systems. If future markets are unhelpful, canny investors need to be that much smarter to make bumper profits. The secret under these tougher conditions is to follow a sound investment plan, like *Backing Winners*, which is designed to do precisely that.

Not all commentators are as gloomy as David Schwartz. Charles Kadlec in *Dow 100,000: Fact or Fiction** is patently an outright optimist. He predicts around two decades of above-average economic growth underpinned by technological advances. These will accelerate productivity improvements and foster dramatic declines in communication costs to produce a truly global marketplace in every imaginable product, including, of course, communications itself. By 2020 the world would have experienced a period of outstanding business opportunities, swiftly rising living standards and immense expansion in world trade possibilities. I see this type of prosperity emerging from the rapid evolution of the Network Economy, where a dense maze of light-based network interconnections circling the planet enables people anywhere on earth to be in touch with family, friends, business partners, clients or suppliers in seconds. The FTSE 100 equivalent of Dow 100,000 would lift it to about 50,000 by 2020, to produce a ten-bagger rise from the 5,000 level of June 2002. Demographic calculations support projections for a continuing stock market boom, as 'forty-somethings' save for retirement over the next decade.

> *'Buy and hold' have replaced 'I love you' as the three most popular words in the English language*
>
> Jim Grant, founder of *Grant's Financial Publishing*

Go for growth

Whenever two investors meet, the chances are their views will be wildly different. In fact, the mindset of investors is deeply split between optimists, convinced the markets will rise, and pessimists, forever searching for the black cloud behind every silver lining. Investment splits are also present between two important

*Charles Kadlec, *Dow 100,000: Fact or Fiction*, Prentice Hall Press, 1999.

investment styles – value or growth. Value investors search for undervalued bargains, keen to buy one pound for 50 pence; growth investors are willing to pay more if the company is set on a fast-growth path. This clash of views becomes a buying opportunity: in falling markets or outright panic when share prices plunge, alert growth investors can pick up choice prospects at discounts.

Value investing thrives in difficult market conditions or during a global economic downturn such as occurred in 2000 and 2001 but it was unpopular during the boom years of 1995 to 2000. Most fund managers were then great advocates of growth investing, as it is easier to find growing companies that are prospering famously. Mike Bishop, head of pan-European equities at Morley Fund Management suggests unpopular companies trade at bargain basement prices because they have low growth prospects. He agrees value investing is a safe haven in turbulent markets but a growth strategy must be better for long-run success. When markets hit a downward trend, smart investors who are following the fortunes of favourite companies may pick up shares at bargain basement prices. This is the best way to combine value and growth investing, especially if the goal is to find profitable ten-baggers. When you pay modest prices, it is easier to reach ten-bagger size, giving you a double benefit.

Self-confidence is the first requisite to great undertakings

Samuel Johnson, author of *A Dictionary of the English Language*

Ten-year targets

Although everyone invests for financial security each of us has a personal approach to creating and holding a share portfolio. Depending on whether one is traditionally cautious or more adventurous, risk attitudes vary especially as age and circumstances change. A forty-year-old family man may plan to save, but bringing up children and repaying a mortgage may restrict his possibilities. Someone nearing retirement will feel far more cautious than a twenty-year-old wanting to buy a car or save for holidays or a down payment on a flat.

My portfolio has been built from experience gained over the past twelve years, but it also rests on memories of what happened to shares between 1972 and 1974 when prices across the whole market sank dramatically over two and a half years, losing 74 per cent of their value. For long-term investors holding their portfolios before and right through the prolonged decline, this interlude proved little more than a short blip but as I began investing relatively late, my experiences are coloured by that shocking decline, by my reading and what I have learned from other investors. In 1990 I set out as a hectic day trader, long before that phrase had even been invented. I frequently (too frequently I now realise) sold shares to lock in profits whenever the news deteriorated and, recalling steep price collapses in the turbulent 1970s, I thought surely this scare marks the end of the bull market. Surprisingly, there were many panics during the 1990s; in August 1992, with the exchange rate fiasco during John Major's government; in February 1994 when Alan Greenspan, chairman of the US central bank, the Federal Reserve Board, raised interest rates unexpectedly and prices plunged; throughout 1994 up to the spring of 1995 markets sank. I sold Perpetual in the spring of 1994 at 1,200p only to watch it rise to 3,000p over the next couple of years without ever being smart enough to decide when was the right moment to buy it back, and at what price. Then again in August 1998, I was a committed seller when the international financial crisis looked really bleak. Russia defaulted on its debts and the currencies of emerging economies were in crisis. In October 1998 I could have repurchased my Sage Group shares at 100p, the price I had sold them at earlier that year – but I hesitated and that opportunity passed.

Learning from these personal experiences I have now built a

portfolio where I feel comfortable holding my shares for a much longer period to give them time to fulfil the early promise that tempted me to buy them initially. Although Jesse Livermore was a dedicated speculator in the early twentieth century, making and losing several fortunes, he did offer this brilliant advice: 'The biggest profits come from sitting, not trading.' Did he know that two-thirds of the gains from holding shares come from reinvested dividends, which is far more difficult to do if you are trading, not sitting? You are bound to miss many of the appropriate cut-off dividend dates if you take a short-term view, which means forfeiting those valuable dividends. Evidence reveals most investors are too impatient to allow the big profits to arrive. Short-term volatility is unimportant for building long-term wealth: a far more sensible plan is to focus on the long-term targets – turning £10,000 into £100,000 in ten years.

History shows the underlying trend has been up for more than one hundred years. Yes, there were two major crashes, in 1929 and 1987, a shocking creeping crash from 1972 to December 1974 plus several smaller panics, including October 1989 and October 1998. Then there were numerous phases when very little happened and markets simply drifted. Yet despite this patchy history, the evidence strongly implies that markets will recover without me being too active either by selling too soon or buying too often. We have to ask ourselves if we think the twentieth century was special or if global economic growth will continue in future more or less as in the past. While the road ahead could be just as unpredictable as that of the twentieth century, astute investors can still make bumper profits by backing winners.

Evidence produced by the investment bank Credit Suisse First Boston is a clinching argument for taking the long view. A twenty-year investment of £100 in the UK stock market in 1980 would by the end of 1999 have grown to £3,833; an impressive result. But if the investor had missed out on the ten best weeks, his return would have nearly halved to £2,028. This massive drop in performance arises because most of the time the market drifts around indecisively. The FTSE 100 index had been doing this from 1999 until the spring of 2001 when it suddenly fell sharply. This abrupt drop was a typical example of a fundamental pattern in market behaviour: occasionally it makes large jumps concentrated into very short periods. If these jumps are up investors on the sidelines miss their profitable chances as no one knows when they are due.

A journey of a thousand miles begins with a single step
Lao-tzu, Chinese philosopher, founder of Taoism

Keep backing winners

A brief look at my early ability to pick superb stocks such as Sage Group, the accountancy software company, and Perpetual, the fund management group, without gaining the maximum benefits underlines the long-term investment message yet again.

Investing in Sage Group, the most profitable share of the 1990s, when it was a tiny, unknown company showed that my FASTER GAINS system for uncovering good prospects could be highly effective. FASTER GAINS was extensively covered in my earlier investment books, *The Armchair Investor* and *The Wealthy Investor*. It does get one airing again in Chapter 7 for new recruits. FASTER GAINS covers eleven key factors, some of which are obviously important for finding and backing winners, so we will look at those winning factors in Chapter 2. But finding winning companies is only a part-strategy. You have to know how to let the profits run and not be shaken out of successful investments by trivial events or market setbacks, until the gains materialise. Sage soared 28,000 per cent in the 1990s since its flotation in 1989.

I first spotted Sage Group in December 1991 when I had been investing for only about a year. I was on to a brilliant winner, but as an inexperienced novice working alone at home I did not adopt a buy-and-hold strategy to enjoy the best gains: I bought shares on three separate occasions and sold them, considerably reducing my profits. The high levels of debt Sage incurred in buying acquisitions to expand its client base worried me in the late 1990s. Large debts make me nervous about future prospects, but what has to be set against the debts is the ability to churn out cash from regular operations. The two elements must be judged together, which I failed to do when assessing Sage's progress.

Initially, however, my only guide was my newly devised mnemonic FASTER GAINS, with which I checked Sage's excellent final results, the day after they were announced early in December. I decided on a small purchase of shares but the advisory broker at the high street bank that we still bank with was most scathing when I rang to place my order. 'Why buy shares in a tin-pot outfit like that? We are strongly recommending Tiphook this month.'

I had never heard of Tiphook, but on checking, I learned it was a ship-transportation company with enormous debts. I often wondered subsequently what happened to Tiphook, until at a talk in September 1999, I related this story and a helpful investor in the audience provided the answers. Yes, Tiphook was a fantastic company in the early 1990s before it hit trading difficulties. He admitted ruefully to having lost £8,000 by remaining invested in Tiphook. His story illustrates that long-term investing comes with a caution: we should reassess companies that hit a bad patch, lose their way, or issue profit warnings.

Back in December 1991 the assertive broker was intimidating and I spent almost the whole day wondering how to buy those Sage shares. Around 3.30 p.m., I plucked up the courage to phone again and was fortunately connected to a different broker; but the delay meant I had to pay around 30p more for each share.

In December 1991 Sage had a market capitalisation of around £250 million. By September 1999 when it entered the FTSE 100 list, its market value was an astonishing £3.5 billion. At that date it was rising in great leaps as the euphoric tide of the millennium boom moved on towards the full flood. Even after the savage fall-out of high technology shares during 2000, its value by August 2001 still exceeded £2.7 billion. And who can say how much additional growth it will achieve during its second decade as a listed company now it has joined Britain's top-ranking businesses?

Sadly, I didn't hold on to my initial purchase of Sage. The second purchase is chronicled in Chapter 9 of *The Armchair Investor*, with a point-by-point explanation of using FASTER GAINS to analyse small growth companies. That analysis for *The Armchair Investor* was prepared in 1996, but I believe Sage remains an excellent FASTER GAINS candidate. Its long-term prospects still look attractive. While FASTER GAINS is helpful for finding attractive small companies with a low risk profile, finding and backing winners is only part of the strategy for success. Knowing how to spot and remove losers is as pivotal as having the patience and foresight to stay with winning companies you do discover. For me, selling out prematurely was an Achilles heel in my investment skills – until I became a long-term investor.

The man who makes no mistakes does not usually make anything

Edward John Phelps, American lawyer and diplomat

Sadly, I repeated this losing strategy with my holding of Perpetual, the fund management group I discovered in mid-1993, years before it became another superb ten-bagger company. With unfortunate timing, Perpetual floated on the UK stock market at 100p a few months before the October 1987 crash. The shares collapsed to around 45p before beginning a recovery with the stock market's revival several months later. Indeed, Perpetual became a recovery stock, an excellent example of a company falling out of favour with investors because it was in a sector (fund management) which became unpopular in the post-October 1987 crash period and had poor prospects as investors shunned the markets. The FTSE 100 index took two years to regain its October 1987 levels, but fund management groups tend to outperform the market. The shares of Perpetual were never subdivided into smaller units as often happens with shares that cost over £10 each. We can therefore see what an excellent investment it was during its whole life as an independent business. From its 45p low the shares reached 3,697p in 2000, rising 8,115 per cent over thirteen years. But this capital gain ignores the truly handsome annual dividends.

I bought 1,000 shares in Perpetual at 345p in spring 1993. When I sold them in spring 1994 at 1,200p they had risen nearly 250 per cent. Amvescap, a larger fund management group bought Perpetual in December 2000. If I had held the shares until that takeover, my £3,450 investment would have grown to £36,970 before adding in the dividends. For 1993 the dividend was 15p (£150 on 1,000 shares): by 2000 it had reached 86p (£860 on my 1,000 shares) for a total dividend payout from 1993 to 2000 of £4,470. The dividends alone would have exceeded my original investment by over £1,000!

This tale shows why investors should be patient when they are fortunate enough to find little gems with fantastic prospects. When I first bought Perpetual shares, the company was worth £98 million. Eight years later Amvescap paid £1.05 billion to acquire it.

Of course, regret over lost opportunities is relative. My too-hasty sales of Sage Group and Perpetual fall into context when set beside the tale of Simo Vuorilehto, Nokia's interim chief executive from 1988 to 1989. On being replaced by Jorma Ollila he sold a large block of Nokia shares to buy a yacht. When Nokia's share price soared to amazing heights in the late 1990s, he realised his mistake, acknowledging that 'I have the world's most expensive yacht.'

Climb the learning curve

Today my portfolio has shed some of my shares in high-risk technology companies. I now hold large blocks by value in slower-growing major FTSE 100 companies that regularly pay high dividends. Balancing your assets is discussed in Chapter 5. In my early days I was guilty of overtrading, and although it made exciting reading for my *Mail on Sunday* diary, it was counterproductive for growing bumper profits. In fact, I believe trading made it harder to grow my wealth. I was also far too impatient with my winning stock-picks, selling them too soon in many cases. By mid-November 2001, with Sage at 262p, my 1995 investment would have been worth £52,400, although values fluctuate with price movements, a more than sevenfold gain in six years on my original investment of £6,380. As my experience clearly shows, a proven strategy to uncover ten-bagger shares falls far short of a total strategy; a disciplined complete plan including a formula for offloading losers is equally important. The investment books I have written, and indeed my daily diary on www.mrscohen.com were intended to share this experience with others, in the hope that it might help them avoid some of my costly errors.

The journey is the reward

Steve Jobs, co-founder of Apple Computer

Target success

Every investor should evaluate at an early stage exactly what he or she wants from holding long-term assets. Are you planning to sell your house every few years, to reinvest the gains after making improvements? I have a cousin who did that over two decades moving up the housing ladder in great leaps and making profits, but I could never have copied him as I prefer a settled life.

The ten-bagger portfolio boosts your chances of building long-term wealth with a starting sum of as little as £5,000 but preferably £10,000. Use this initial fund to choose ten promising companies for a ten-bagger portfolio to hold for ten years.

There are very few rules to ensure success, but above all you must have patience to allow your system to prove itself. This is easier if you have a vision of future goals. Try to avoid being tempted with risky short cuts such as following newspaper tips or ignoring the long-term targets you have set yourself. Avoid taking high risks by fitting each new investment choice into the big picture of your total portfolio, covering as wide a spread of different sectors as possible.

Learn as you go along by refining the edges to boost your chances of success. Turn your investment programme into a hobby for life and it will repay you many times over. Even better, it will pay for all your other hobbies – world cruises, holiday homes, collecting rare books, antique furniture among other favourites.

Backing Winners outlines a profitable and focused investment system that is eminently suitable for all investors, whether experienced or novices. It needs only a modest initial outlay, to form one element in a total investment scheme. Target success and think in tens: *ten* steps to success from a portfolio of *ten* possible *ten*-baggers, to hold for *ten* years. Adopt the full concept, follow the guidelines and give the strategy time to work.

Target the tens

1. Follow the Ten-point Action Plan
2. Avoid the Ten most common investment mistakes
3. Spend Ten months to one year finding suitable candidates
4. Create a Ten-bagger portfolio
5. Stock it with your Ten most exciting prospects
6. Set a target to turn Ten thousand pounds into £100,000
7. Rely on the Ten most important reasons for selling losers early

8. Hold the portfolio for at least Ten years
9. Learn as you go so you can hold your portfolio for another Ten years
10. Grow the portfolio another Tenfold, turning £100,000 into £1 million

Are you ready to begin? Then we can start exploring profiles of winning companies in Chapter 2.

To improve is to change; to be perfect is to change often

Winston Churchill

2 **Profile of a Ten-bagger**

Genius is one per cent inspiration and ninety-nine per cent perspiration

Thomas Edison, inventor and founder of General Electric

The top three American companies vary each year but in 2000 all were growth-oriented with two in high technology sectors. General Electric, an old-fashioned conglomerate, was top; second was Microsoft, with its huge monopoly on computer operating systems, and third was Cisco Systems, the leading Internet infrastructure equipment manufacturer. Even after steep price falls over 2000 and 2001, GE and Microsoft were still in the top three in 2001, joined by Exxon Mobil, an oil group, operating in a vital industry for a scarce commodity. These are truly gigantic organisations: GE had a market capitalisation of $415 billion, Microsoft $348 billion and Exxon Mobil $285 billion in August 2001. In the UK the three largest companies by market value listed on the London Stock Exchange in August 2001 were oil giant BP, which announced its biggest profits ever in August; second was GlaxoSmithKline, the drugs group, with Vodafone, the mobile telecoms group, third. In August 2001 BP was worth £132 billion, GlaxoSmithKline £120 billion and Vodafone £100 billion.

Pursuing growth

Most future ten-baggers will be small, unknown companies when you find them, but as they are highly risky, knowing the stages through which most companies grow is helpful. To ensure continuing success, growth strategies must prosper: it sounds abundantly obvious, but in practice this message can get blurred or ignored. Periodic setbacks or economic downturns must be well managed if the company's growth plans are to stay on track. Moreover, the majority of small companies grow large and even more profitable by acquiring other smaller rivals. The acquisitions activity can literally make or break the future progress of growing companies: it can be their Achilles heel, as we shall see in Chapter 3 with Marconi, or their route to amazing profitability, as it was for Sage Group. The table below outlines the main phases of growth that many companies undergo.

If your mind is empty, it is always ready for anything; it is open to everything

Shunryu Suzuki, Japanese Zen priest and teacher

How companies grow

1. Early start-up phase supported by founders, venture capitalists or a bank
2. Alternatively, a company may be floated off (demerged) from a larger parent
3. Profits emerge
4. Expansion plans are devised
5. Bolt-on acquisitions are made to existing businesses
6. Diversifications may be introduced, unrelated to core businesses
7. Periodic setbacks must be well managed to maintain growth
8. New blockbuster products are introduced
9. A new chief executive gives growth an added boost
10. Maturity sets in and growth flattens out

The merger trail

For a company to grow from small to ten-bagger size something pretty huge has to happen. It may have a winning formula for producing niche goods that become a mass-consumer product with universal appeal, as happened in the 1980s with personal computers and in the late 1990s with mobile phones. It may have a blockbuster product that other competitors cannot match, as with Glaxo's ulcer treatment Zantac, or Microsoft's monopoly-commanding Windows operating systems. But for most modest firms the route to gigantism is through mergers and acquisitions. However, plenty of evidence suggests many mergers and acquisitions do not achieve the ambitious goals that managers set. Outcomes tend to be disappointing, although as in everything financial, there are exceptions. Jack Welch, the admired chief executive of America's titan General Electric, was a consummate deal-maker with an enviable record of successfully integrating acquisitions.

Big thrusts in mergers and acquisitions come in waves, geared to the business and stock market cycle, with most activity at the peak of the boom. The reason is easily explained; many acquisitions, especially hostile bids to take over a firm against the wishes of its incumbent management, involve acquiring an undervalued target by using the company's own overvalued currency, its rising share price. In many cases, no cash is involved: they are all-share takeovers. The late 1990s saw a virtual explosion of takeover activity due to a more favourable regulatory environment and the coincidental emergence of the peaking of the prolonged 1990s bull market when soaring share prices of acquiring companies offered irresistible temptation to ambitious bosses to use their inflated shares as the currency for merger and acquisition deals. When the market went into a rapid reverse during 2000, it ushered in a painful period of write-downs and grossly weakened balance sheets, to reflect the fallen values of these expensive acquisitions.

High on drugs

Figures show the average person takes more drugs in the last year of life than in all the others combined. As people will always need medicines, pharmaceutical companies are classed with food retailers and utility firms as 'defensive', compared to 'cyclical' groups, such as transport, banks and travel companies that face problems in recessions. Defensive companies continue growing their profits and revenues during tough trading conditions and can ride out a downturn. The discovery of a new blockbuster drug can transform the prospects for a small pharmaceutical firm. This happened to Glaxo (before its 1995 merger with Wellcome and the 2000 merger with SmithKline Beecham). In the 1980s Glaxo benefited from the enormous selling potential of Zantac, a treatment for stomach (peptic) ulcers. Among Glaxo's great strengths are its superb marketing skills and large sales force, especially strong in America, an important and profitable market. Tagamet, a rival drug with similar properties, was produced by SmithKline and French (as it was known before the Beecham takeover), yet Glaxo's focused selling techniques swept Zantac to the top treatment favoured by doctors, enabling Glaxo to earn huge profits. On the back of impressive Zantac sales Glaxo became a ten-bagger during the 1980s.

Champions know that success is inevitable
Conrad Hilton, hotelier and founder of Hilton Hotels

In 1983 I met a retired nurse on an evening course we both attended. When she invited me to lunch I met her husband, a retired oil engineer, who was ecstatic about his investment in Glaxo and its fabulous dividends. As I vaguely recall, this information scarcely impressed me although his enthusiasm certainly did. Perhaps my expression was as blank as the glassy look on my husband's face in December 1991, when I told him we had made a £6,000 profit on

Glaxo shares within two tax-free Personal Equity Plans (Peps), in fourteen months. In 1983 Glaxo was on a swift flight-path to ten-bagger status. I bought my original Glaxo shares in September 1990 at the equivalent of about £7, after allowing for share splits. The shares have achieved a near twofold rise since then but, yes, you guessed it, I sold in February 1992 at £9 only to reinvest in 1997 when I had to pay around £12.70 for my new holding. Following the merger with SmithKline Beecham my shares in the new group GlaxoSmithKline must leap to £127 to be a ten-bagger, surely an impossible task. But consider the dividend attractions, which for Glaxo rose from 0.2p in 1972 to 0.8p by 1982, 17p by 1991 and 39p in 2001. Five share splits from 1972 grew 1,000 shares into 32,000 by simply holding, to give rising annual dividends from £2 in 1972 to £12,480 in 2001 on a holding worth £540,000.

Even gigantic companies might become ten-baggers if they are still enjoying explosive growth. We can look at Dell Computer, General Electric or Nokia for clues on how they thrive.

Visionary bosses

Without a focused stock picking system, the chances of outperforming the market do not look encouraging, but backing companies with strong bosses, a powerful product and niche markets can turn a modest portfolio into a successful one simply by staying with the companies that pursue a focused approach to their core businesses.

I, personally, don't see any reason why we can't capture as much as 40 per cent of the customer opportunity that exists out there in the market

Michael Dell, founder and chief executive of Dell Computer

The role of a visionary boss cannot be overestimated: some

become famous as the founders and driving force behind success. We immediately think of Bill Gates, Walt Disney and Richard Branson but one stunning example is Michael Dell, the 36-year-old founder and chief executive of the company which bears his name. Keeping customers happy has been his central credo since he founded Dell in 1984 with $1,000 while still a student at the University of Texas. Early in 2001 Dell became the largest manufacturer of personal computers, having overtaken archrival Compaq, although the merger of Compaq with Hewlett-Packard subsequently shot the merged group to the top position, Dell has grown to become a leader in its field by running an extremely lean operation, based on direct computer selling, pioneered by Michael Dell. Initially, telephone sales dominated but increasingly the company has come to sell via the Internet, with half its business transacted online by 2001. More impressively, Dell gained market share as global PC sales declined through forcing down its own costs without damaging its margins too much and imposing an aggressive price war which attracted buyers away from less nimble competitors. Profits after tax in 2000 were $2.3 billion, a rise of 24 per cent on 1999. The secret recipe for attracting sales worth $32 billion involved cutting out intermediaries, keeping production lean and focusing heavily on customer service, with products built to order, so that only four days of inventory needs to be held, far less than rivals. Dell is fanatical about customer benefits, which translate into market share, profits and growth.

In an interview with the *Financial Times* during tough trading times in 2001, he made clear his determination to give his rivals no quarter: 'We're profitable, we're growing, and it's sort of crunch time for our competitors because they are in a commodity business. They can't differentiate themselves, even among themselves, and certainly not against Dell, and they're losing money. So they've got tough choices to make.' It was not clear then whether Dell's aggressive pricing and relentless cost-cutting could keep it ahead when PCs have become commodity products and IT companies have to mutate their business models frequently to stay ahead of the new Internet-driven business environment.

The house that Jack built

Jack Welch ranks among the world's most admired bosses; he made history in 2001 when he stepped down as chief executive of General Electric after twenty years at the helm, having spent his whole working life in the company. He masterminded an effective acquisitions policy that grew the century-old US titan from around $14 billion in 1981 to $419 billion by 2001. Under his stewardship, $100 invested in GE from 1980 to 1999 reached $7,183 compared to $2,339 for the same sum invested in the Dow Jones Industrial Average. Even given that he had taken over a thriving prosperous business, by his retirement GE was financially more powerful than many independent nation states. As well as being a superb deal-maker, Jack Welch was a single-minded leader driven to win. He powered the business forward and higher, up the market capitalisation stakes until it became the most valuable company in America, a stunning achievement.

GE is big and it's going to get bigger

Jack Welch at GE's AGM, April 2001

When he became boss of General Electric's empire in the early 1980s, the world was suffering a severe recession and the core GE business centred on a group of manufactured goods – diesel locomotives, jet engines, high-technology diagnostic medical equipment, transformers, plastics, power systems and portable lighting. Conglomerates such as GE became unpopular in the 1990s but GE defied the logic of unfocused diversification because its laser-focused chief executive more than amply compensated.

His vision was to grow GE faster and bigger than ever before through two early attacks on the bureaucracy inherent in almost every large company. Before he had been one full year in charge, he announced that all businesses had to be first or second in their sector; if not, they would be disbanded. The second plank involved a huge cost-cutting programme, eliminating 80,000 jobs, which earned him the derogatory nickname 'neutron Jack', implying he obliterated people while leaving buildings standing. He then implemented four growth initiatives, globalisation, product service, Six Sigma (a quality improvement programme) and digitalisation, to counter threats posed by dotcom upstarts. His revolutionary measures to propel GE along a faster growth trajectory were achieved by laying stronger foundations. He imagined that an enormous company can act like its far smaller rivals and wanted GE to be able to grow like a smaller, nifty company, despite its exploding size. By his retirement GE had achieved group-wide operating margins of 19 per cent.

The role of GE is growth and we have been able to prove that the bigger we are, the faster we can grow

Jeffrey Immelt, successor to Jack Welch, September 2001

His entrepreneurial management style turned conventional investment strategy upside down: while every other conglomerate concern was broken up and dispersed in the 1980s and 1990s, under Jack Welch GE grew at a formidable pace. By his retirement, GE Capital, the financial division, represented about 40 per cent of GE's consolidated net earnings. Bob Nardelli, a former GE Capital board member, described it as 'a tremendous arrow in the quiver'. The financial subsidiaries cover a wide range of operations, including consumer credit cards, insurance and trailer leasing. Jeanne Terrile of Merrill Lynch pointed out, 'GE is many things but it is not overpoweringly any one thing so it is hard to find an appropriate set of comparable companies against which to test GE's valuation.'

Powering-up General Electric

1981, April: Ron Jones retires and is succeeded by Jack Welch, aged forty-five, as chairman and chief executive

1981, December: Welch announces that all GE businesses must be first or second in their sector. If not they faced being disbanded

1985, December: $6.3 billion takeover of RCA, entertainment (NCB) and consumer electronics

1986, April: GE takes control of Kidder Peabody, the investment bank

1987, July: GE sells consumer electronics unit to Thompson of France and takes control of Thompson's medical equipment subsidiary

Mid-1980s:* 'Globalisation' begins, the first of Welch's four 'growth initiatives'

1988, September: Welch begins country-wide 'work-out' process with staff tackling problems

Late 1995:* 'Product service' initiative focuses on generating revenues from installed product base and improving efficiency for customers

1996, January:* GE adopts the 'Six Sigma' quality improvement programme

1999, January:* Welch launches 'digitalisation' as reaction to the dotcom threat

2000, October: Welch masterminds $43 billion bid for Honeywell and delays his retirement

2001, July: European Commission blocks Honeywell bid on competition grounds, aborting what would have been the world's largest industrial takeover

2001, 7 September: Jack Welch retires and is succeeded by Jeffrey Immelt, aged forty-five, as chairman and chief executive

*Growth initiatives – four in total.

2001, 14 September: GE issues a profit warning over estimated $600 million of insurance claims linked to the World Trade Center disaster

2001, 21 September: GE announces it is on course for 11 per cent growth in earnings for the current year

I was chairman for two days; I had an airplane with my engines [in it] hit a building I insured, covered by a network I owned [NBC] – and I still [expect to] increase earnings by 11 per cent

Jeffrey Immelt, newly appointed chairman of GE, speaking on 21 September 2001

Nokia – the next Microsoft?

Is there anyone on the planet who has not heard of Nokia? In spring 1987 chief executive Kari Kairamo was interviewed by the *Wall Street Journal*, which to judge by one caustic comment, was definitely not expecting ten-baggers in Finland. 'Like its homeland, Nokia has an image problem. Outside of Finland it barely has one.'

Although Nokia's global presence is fairly recent, the company is almost 140 years old. In the nineteenth century Nokia was the name of a small mill and river less than ten miles from Tampere, a major Finnish industrial city. After such remarkable longevity, Nokia has had a chequered history, reinventing itself several times, passing through numerous conglomerate phases before the mobile operations emerged. Nokia is an astonishing European success story that demonstrates incredible survivorship qualities. In a book about the company, *The Nokia Revolution*,* Dan Steinbock records how Nokia learned to value vision, flexibility and key strategic decisions.

In the 1960s Nokia's telecommunications and radio-phones

*Dan Steinbock, *The Nokia Revolution*, New York, Amacom, 2001.

formed one insignificant division: the focus on mobile phones began in the late 1980s and early 1990s, coinciding with the collapse of Communism and Soviet trade and a severe recession in Finland. This marked a turning point in the fortunes of Finland and its most prestigious multinational business, Nokia, which are now both increasingly interlinked.

In 1982 Nokia's market value was around $9 billion: by spring 1987, as the flagship of Finnish industry, it had 27,600 employees and a market capitalisation of $27 billion, a threefold growth in five years. In the *Wall Street Journal* interview Kairamo explained, 'Nokia wants to forget being a Finnish company and become more Scandinavian, more European.' This was his vision but the *Wall Street Journal* was unimpressed, denigrating the lack of image, which Nokia was intent on aggressively addressing. By focusing on global branding, its success is now undeniable. Sadly, within eighteen months of the interview, both chief executive and his favoured successor were dead. Another crisis loomed.

After 800 years, [Finland] an overnight success
Newsweek headline, 21 June 1999

Yet between the end of 1998 and April 2000, Nokia's market capitalisation rose from $73 billion to $250 billion in one giant bound. In eighteen years the company enjoyed a phenomenal growth, from $9 billion to $250 billion, a rise of 2,678 per cent. Despite adversity in 1989, Nokia became a formidable ten-bagger and still seems capable of exploiting the next wave of innovative technologies, mobile Internet and broadband network systems.

In 2001 CEO Jorma Ollila's contract was extended through to 2006, to enable the group to manage successfully the tricky transition to third generation technology. Early in January 2002 he celebrated ten years at the helm of Nokia. During that tenure, the shares had risen 164-fold in euros and 108-fold in dollars; its market capitalisation at around €126 billion ($77 billion) was only slightly lower than the total gross domestic product for its country of origin, Finland. Ollila personally felt confident about Nokia's future, and relaxed about the challenges ahead, 'We have tremendous strengths. We just have to keep implementing well.'

Ten-bagger titans

Having looked briefly at the driving force behind Dell Computer and GE's spectacular growth, this brief glimpse of Nokia's remarkable progress leads us to the concept of ten key factors to identify ten-bagger winners. Like a novelist checking through earlier novels for a formula to discover the elusive bestseller, we can list the essential features of these gigantic businesses as a profile to recognise potential future winners. The vital checklist we shall be following applies to Dell, GE or many other companies, but here we shall use Nokia to illustrate the key features to look for:

Identity pointers to Ten-baggers

1. Visionary chief executive with a sound business plan
2. Operates in a market with huge future growth potential
3. Niche market with high entry costs to deter competitors
4. Opportunity to be the leading company in its sector
5. Highly cash generative products and cash in the bank
6. Low debt levels
7. Potential to build a powerful brand
8. Large and expanding pool of contracts, clients, markets
9. Not dependent solely on one key product, market or client
10. Ability to evolve and develop new innovative products

It is better to lead than to follow

Carly Fiorina, chairman & chief executive, Hewlett-Packard

Ten-bagger profile of Nokia

Visionary chief executive with a sound business plan

One proven route to expand your wealth from stock market investing is to back an ambitious and energetic entrepreneur who has dedicated most of his working life to building up a business. Among Britain's dedicated entrepreneurs are Lord Harris of Carpetright, Charles Dunstone of Carphone Warehouse and Martyn Arbib who built Perpetual.

The chief executives who masterminded Nokia's meteoric rise are not globally famous but they were the driving force for Nokia's ambitions since the 1960s. Dan Steinbock attributes Nokia's 'third incarnation' to Kari Kairamo, who ran the conglomerate during its 'investment phase' until his untimely death in December 1988. (Nokia subsequently embarked upon its current 'innovative phase'.) From Kairamo's time as managing director in 1977 and while he was CEO from 1986, he endeavoured to stay one or two steps ahead of public policies and company strategies, positioning Nokia for growth in new markets and emerging industries. He led by personal example and a tenacious persistence that often produced maverick behaviour, described by Kairamo himself as 'management by *perkele* [Satan]'. Dan Steinbock notes, 'Nokia's current CEO, Jorma Ollila, is highly respected, but Kairamo, a charismatic and passionate leader, was loved.' Both chief executives had great people skills, faced challenges eagerly, and had a radiant vision for Nokia's future.

Kairamo's vision focused on shaping Nokia into an international high-growth technology giant. He was obsessed with the need to influence mobile standards and increase market share. Change and flexibility became priorities and Nokia was an early convert to the new business philosophy of competitive advantage (creating shareholder value by being a leader in a chosen field), to replace the old ideas of comparative advantage (relying on the benefits of existing internally generated natural resources). During the 1970s and 1980s Kairamo looked to the stunning growth of Japanese companies. They have subsequently lost momentum in a decade-long economic malaise that has paralysed Japan. Before their loss of dynamism, Kairamo's vision encompassed 'a kind of Japanese model', as he, like thousands of astute observers around the world, saw Japan's economy as the great success of the 1980s. As Kairamo urged, 'We must learn to become fast.' In his vision of the future, 'If one isn't fast enough in the most competitive segments of electronics, there just aren't any chances to succeed.'

Operates in a market with huge future growth potential

In June 2001 EMC World Cellular Database forecast, based on actual figures to end March, that by year-end world cellular subscriptions would exceed 1 billion, up from 728 million at year-end 2000. Although subscription growth in western Europe had slowed, in the rest of the world, especially Latin America and the Asia-Pacific regions, it continued increasing. EMC assumed some markets would grow beyond 100 per cent saturation, implying consumers can own more than one mobile phone. They could become ubiquitous items especially if m-commerce (mobile commerce) usage explodes. People could use their mobiles to buy goods and pay for them on their mobile accounts, treating them like credit or debit cards. This is one of the major mobile expansions industry insiders are relying on for huge future growth. EMC forecast world subscriber growth would double to 2 billion by 2004, while in Africa and the Middle East growth rates could more than double. But as Nokia foresaw during the 1980s, the greatest cash bonanza should come from China's 1.3 billion people, as increasing numbers become mobile subscribers. By mid-2001, when Vodafone, the world's largest global mobile operator had about 95 million subscribers, China had 167 million fixed-line telephone subscribers and 121 million mobile subscribers, making it the largest cellular phone market in the world and still at the start of a decade-long explosion in users. BDA, a Beijing-based consultancy, predicts 370 million mobile subscribers in China by 2005.

Niche market with high entry costs to deter competitors

By mid-2001 mobile phone industry casualties reflected the global economic slowdown. Philips of the Netherlands was considering closing its phone division, US-based Motorola, Sweden's Ericsson and Germany's Siemens were reporting losses in their handset divisions. But Nokia's interim results, announced in July, showed market share had soared to 35 per cent. Profits had increased although it forecast slower growth ahead. Yet on announcing full-year results in January 2002, Nokia confounded the sceptics. Despite the global economic downturn it had increased its market share in handset sales for the full year to 37.5 per cent, up from 32 per cent a year previously, with fourth quarter sales reaching almost 40 per cent of the market. This heroic result was achieved at the expense of all its competitors. Nokia remained optimistic about future growth, predicting global handset sales would recover to around 420 million to 440 million for 2002, up from 380 million in 2001.

> *Fast and focused, with a canny eye on design, Nokia wrested market share from entrenched competitors and emerged as the most profitable player in the industry*
>
> *Business Week*, August 1998

The real battle, however, was about to begin, with the development of sophisticated handsets, always-on wireless Internet technology and upgrades to third-generation (3G) networks, all involving hugely expensive research and development costs to deter new entrants, although several major competitors are working to make 3G technology a reality for mobile phone customers.

Opportunity to be the leading company in its sector

By mid-2001, with a glut of new phones and demand shrinking, several mobile phone manufacturers were restructuring. Jorma Ollila thought companies needed a market share of between 7 to 10 per cent to weather the economic cycles and carry the burden of brand marketing plus research and development. Nokia had ousted Motorola, which had been the undisputed leading mobile handset producer in the mid-1990s, and overtaken the second largest producer, Ericsson, to establish its lead position and was well placed to retain that first mover advantage.

Highly cash generative products and cash in the bank

Rapid growth has turned mobile phones from luxury items into a mass produced commodity, but Nokia's proven record in cost-control and managing working capital helped it through the 2000–2001 downturn. Strong profits reported in third-quarter results in October showed Nokia was managing the slowdown better than its rivals. Jorma Ollila predicted a rise in fourth-quarter global handset shipments from 94 million in the third to 110 million, but over 10 million down on the final quarter of 2000. Nokia had achieved a 19 per cent profit margin on handsets and generated €1.4 billion (£867.5 million) net cash in the quarter with €3.2 billion (£1.98 billion) on the balance sheet.

Low debt levels

Research and development are major expenses, but Nokia's debt levels were relatively low in 2001 although development work on 3G networks will be hugely expensive.

Potential to build a powerful brand

As we saw, a determined effort to build a global brand occurred during the 1990s. Although Kairamo had realised decades earlier how vital branding would be, building the brand took several years.

Nokia invested almost $1 billion during the 1990s building a global brand. By 2000 Nokia's global brand had become a most valuable asset, ranked fifth in the world by consulting firm Interbrand.

Large and expanding pool of contracts, clients, markets

Over two decades Nokia viewed itself in global growth terms as a small enterprise leveraging its global position by exploiting its vision of competitive advantage over rivals. Nokia's website announces, 'Nokia is the world leader in mobile communications.' It has become the leading supplier of mobile phones and mobile fixed broadband and IP (Internet Protocol) networks and plans to add mobility to the Internet, a huge untapped market for future profitability. One example is location-based services, such as booking a table at a restaurant or theatre tickets via your mobile phone, through m-commerce; another is the downloading of music or video clips on to your mobile or computer games. All these and similar new facilities suggest the extensive range of services that could become the norm within a matter of a few years.

By the mid-1990s Nokia was pursuing a strategy of global focus, already successfully exploited by Coca-Cola. This involved leveraging limited resources by narrowing the business focus while maximising international coverage, described by Jean-Pierre Jeanet, the business guru promoting this approach, as 'achieving a global mindset'. His idea encapsulates creating a business with a global reach despite having limited resources, by adopting a highly focused approach.

When you stop taking risks –
well, you've reached the end of the story
Oliver Stone, film director

Not dependent solely on one key product, market or client

For years Nokia was committed to a long-term development and preferred partnership in China, its second largest market. By mid-2001 $1.7 billion had been invested and Nokia had twenty representative offices, eight joint ventures and an R&D centre with over 5,500 employees there. With its open border policy and vast population, China is forecast to be the second largest economy in the world within a decade. This is the greatest untapped market available to companies producing and marketing mass-consumer products.

Nokia realised at an early date that it was a small enterprise among the competing giants, Motorola and Ericsson. It has therefore turned niche opportunities into an art form, tailoring its strategy to focus on several narrow segments such as the recent teenage love affair with mobiles. Speed, flexibility and swifter responses to consumer needs spearheaded its focused strategy of using limited resources while creating a global market.

Ability to evolve and develop new innovative products

Unlike its larger rivals, Nokia began very early in its mobile development to position itself as a consumer-products company. New models were introduced annually, changing colours to create new fashions, and it encouraged customisation with clip-on covers. The shortening product cycle for mobiles required speed and flexibility plus a focus on research and development for introducing new products. Nokia benefits from its simpler product line with more standardised components so suppliers find it easier to increase or cut back on productions and deliveries. Dan Steinbock stresses the agility Nokia has shown throughout its long history in taking key strategic decisions to focus on new markets and industries. This is part of its proven success and a platform for future developments to keep it in the forefront of innovations for the Network Economy now evolving. A recent example is the way Nokia grew its cellular products from a niche market to a mass-consumer market ahead of its rivals. Nordic teenagers, who called early cumbersome mobile appliances 'yuppy toys', had become mobile addicts by the 1990s, nimbly fingering text messages with new technology, Short Messaging Services (SMS). Their obsessive involvement illustrates how rapidly 'new' technologies can become ubiquitous, an encouraging outlook for the mobile industry which is still in an early stage of development.

This analysis came from several sources: Steinbock's *The Nokia Revolution*, Nokia's website, investment magazines and press reports. No one should consider buying shares in foreign companies without some detective work. Information is now more freely available but investors should be knowledgeable before buying. However, choosing world-beating firms such as Nokia means there will always be articles, without needing to dig too deeply.

Treasure hunting for ten-baggers is one side of a coin. Flip that coin and you expose all the elements that destroy companies, ruin reputations, eliminate jobs and decimate shareholders' wealth. For thousands caught up in disaster stories, this bruising episode has miserable consequences. But the silver lining is that smart investors can use these gruelling lessons to avoid looming future pitfalls. Investors will then recognise warning signs of a failing company whenever they notice executives behaving in the opposite way to ten-bagger bosses.

Bearing this reverse strategy in mind, we can turn to Chapter 3 and learn how to spot losing companies before they decimate our wealth.

Whenever you see a successful business,
someone once made a courageous decision

Peter Drucker, business guru

3 Learning How to Lose

I'll tell you how I became a winner, I learned how to lose

Martin Schwartz, American hedge fund manager

Hunting for ten-baggers is exciting; but knowing how to rescue yourself from a collapsing company is vital for success. The speed with which companies can fall apart is a frightening aspect of modern business, as we will see later in this chapter when we examine the rapid demise of some former stock market favourites. It is imperative that investors stay alert to these shock horror stories and they must be ready to bail out when disaster threatens. My experience with the Polly Peck debacle in 1990 illustrates the pitfalls of staying aboard when a company hits trouble.

We must not, however, confuse a failing company with the general effects of a recession on many if not all companies, or with the way tough economic conditions affect those in one sector with special problems, as was evident for BT and Vodafone in the summer of 2001 when writing down assets bought earlier at excessive prices during the millennium boom resulted in larger than expected losses.

Dreaded profit warnings

A survey by accountants Ernst & Young reported that 236 companies issued profit warnings in the first six months of 2001, with an accelerating trend as fifty warnings were in July alone compared to 100 for the previous three months. One in five of these companies had issued at least one profit warning within the previous year. Their next survey was even gloomier; share prices of companies issuing profit warnings in the third quarter declined on average by 23 per cent on the first day after the warning, with a record number of 135 profit warnings and 150 forecast for the final quarter. Profit warnings often come in groups, some weeks or months apart, a helpful selling signal for investors holding a failing investment.

Ernst & Young quoted several excuses, including livestock diseases (BSE and foot-and-mouth), accounting blunders and rail chaos but the top ten reasons are listed below:

Most commonly reported profit warnings

1. Sales lower than forecast
2. Flat or declining consumer spending
3. Delays in negotiating/signing new contracts
4. Currency issues (strong pound/weak euro/strong dollar)
5. World economic problems (Asia, Brazil, Russia, Japan)
6. Internal management problems, failed systems, etc
7. Cost of mergers and acquisitions
8. Millennium bug issues
9. Poor weather
10. Delays bringing new products to market

Source: Ernst & Young, *The Times*, 8 August 2001

Riding the boom …

For the entire investment community, amateurs and professionals alike, the late 1990s boom was surely a 'once-in-a-lifetime' experience. Maybe some grandchildren in 2025 will ask their grandpas what they did in the millennium boom! The foundations for prosperity seemed robust. In February 2000, America's expansion, that had begun in March 1991, became the longest period of continuous growth in its history; an epic milestone and cause for jubilation.

It was doubly bewildering therefore to be swept up in fantastic euphoria only to taste the bittersweet aftermath of the ensuing drastic price declines. Many novice investors, piling in towards the peak, suffered nasty losses, turning them against future investing, perhaps for years. America's high-tech bubble began long before Britain's copycat surge, so while the US boom unfolded slowly to the unstable peak and decline, the British version was compressed into a few months, from autumn 1999 to March 2000.

Profile of losers

For investors learning how to spot promising companies that stumble, the post-millennium decline, was one of the best schools to attend. A string of disasters appeared in quick succession; investors looking for warning signs of impending failure were spoilt for choice as to which sectors or companies to follow. The best protection is to understand how companies grow, recognise the usual profile of losers and identify signs of trouble early.

Chapter 2 discussed how ten-bagger companies share a cluster of features that set them apart as potential blockbuster successes. By turning the list around we produce a mirror image of characteristics that send failing companies into the spiral of decline that can lead to a financial black hole – suspension, bankruptcy, liquidation. Several key factors identify the losers, but most problems spring from weak, unfocused management executing ill-judged or poorly prepared plans. Slack management controls could conceal fraud, misappropriated funds or inventory build-ups that must be written off or sold at knock-down prices.

The list of ten key factors for losing companies mirrors in reverse the ten-bagger profile discussed in Chapter 2.

Identity pointers to losing companies

1 Unfocused or misguided management with a weak business plan

2 Operates in a mature market with low future growth potential
3 Crowded market with low entry costs and too many competitors
4 Few opportunities to become a leading edge company
5 Not highly cash generative and may undertake a reckless expansion programme
6 Mounting debts
7 Misuse of the brand advantage, often associated with adverse publicity when the company is forced to cope in public with its problems
8 Shrinking market share, numbers of clients or contracts
9 Diversifying into new products or markets instead of focusing on the core business
10 May hit a crisis due to poor management decisions and high debts

There's an old saying: fool me once, shame on you – fool me twice, shame on me

Michael Mandel, economics editor of *Business Week*

Dotcom disasters

The most publicised disaster zone was the abrupt implosion of the dotcom sector (young, start-up companies operating on the world wide web), where millennium exuberance had driven investors to amazing heights of optimism and irrationality. For investors, dotcom companies suddenly became 'must have' investments, at any price. For companies, building websites rapidly became a high priority: even the influential *Financial Times* spent millions building websites where a great deal of previously expensive information was freely available to all Internet visitors.

Subsequently, many dotcoms suffered price declines of over 90 per cent, which is the true definition of a bubble collapse. Some UK groups, such as Clickmango, the health-and-beauty products website, fronted by television star Joanna Lumley, went into voluntary liquidation, returning cash to shareholders following an orderly closure. Others like Freeserve, the UK's largest Internet service provider, split off from parent Dixons, the leading high street computer retailer, were bought by groups with deeper pockets to fund future development. The problem was that the dotcoms were young, untried firms, more suited to private equity funding than trading as public companies after high-profile stock market flotations. The publicity accompanying quotation exposes teething difficulties, magnified by cynical journalists and aggravated by rapid investor disenchantment. When new funding from venture capitalists or investors abruptly dried up, these struggling young companies faced a bleak future. Stock market favourites became pariahs with fiendish abruptness.

Demise of Independent Insurance

During the late 1990s Independent Insurance was a small company with a big reputation for growing profits. It was seen as a dazzling upstart in an area dominated by long-established blue chip rivals. Independent rapidly became a hot favourite with analysts, brokers and investors. The sudden catastrophe that overtook the company in 2001 seemed to be a purely instant disaster. Yet by following the breaking story, investors who bought shares when it was a favourite, fast-growing business showing bumper profits, could have bailed out before the final abrupt share price collapse: but only by being nimble and focused. With the shares suspended investors still aboard lost their entire investment. The collapse of Independent was one of the high-profile failures of 2001, leaving 500,000 policyholders and 40,000 commercial customers, including the London Fire Brigade, seeking alternative cover. Independent faced unquantified losses from claims that were never recorded in its accounting systems, and faced an investigation by the Serious Fraud Office.

A lightning demise is a shocking event. We can follow the

company's fate to see the early warning signals before total collapse locked investors into a bankruptcy situation.

Independent Insurance was floated in November 1993 at the equivalent of 49p, after accounting for later share splits. Reported pre-tax profits were growing strongly in 1996, and rose from £40.2 million to £59.1 million by 1999. During that four-year period earnings per share almost doubled, from 10.3p in 1996 to 18.5p. Over five years the dividend more than doubled, growing from 2.65p in 1996 to 5.75p in 2000, but by February 2001 problems had surfaced. The share price began 2001 at 402p but in February it started on a steep decline in the wake of a steady stream of bad news: it had fallen to 139p by close of trading on 25 May and was suspended at 81.5p on 11 June. The company quickly went into liquidation soon after a rescue rights issue proposal was aborted. Early in August, Michael Bright, charismatic founder and architect of Independent's spectacular rise and equally rapid implosion, was declared bankrupt, with enormous debts.

The sequence of company events that marked this looming collapse turned out to be trailers or milestones, for the forthcoming disaster of suspension followed so speedily by liquidation.

Events in 2001 at Independent Insurance

February: Independent issued a profit warning and discussed with advisers a plan to raise £220 million in a rights issue through an institutional placing

March: Independent announced a massive profits fall for 2000

April: Founder Michael Bright resigned as chief executive

May: Assessors, Watson Wyatt, said it had discovered new, previously undisclosed liabilities

11 June: Shares suspended at 81.5p when Independent Insurance said it was going to raise new capital

14 June: Bright quit as Independent was closed 'temporarily' for new business, conceding the share placing had failed

17 June: Insolvency specialist PriceWaterhouseCoopers informed the board of liabilities up to £220 million greater than reserves
7 August: Michael Bright filed and won a petition for bankruptcy
14 September: Bright's debts to four main creditors amount to £5 million

These events unfolded so rapidly investors had little time to assess the severity of the crisis. One early sign was the increase in the 2000 dividend, almost 20 per cent higher than that of 1999, despite the huge pre-tax profits fall. Was this to reassure investors or purely overconfidence? Figures showed the company pursued a generous dividend policy. When founder executives hold large blocks of shares high dividends are attractive annual benefits. Michael Bright owned 6.18 per cent of the equity in June 2001, a substantial holding.

People with too many choices rarely make the right ones
Dr John Blaine, psychologist, University of Southern California

Insecurity at Baltimore Technologies

Baltimore Technologies, the Irish Internet security company, was one of the UK's great white hopes in the high-tech boom as a pioneer in Internet security software, an auxiliary sector supporting dotcom companies. By summer 2000 Baltimore was busy integrating its latest and largest acquisition, Content Technologies, an American e-mail security group, when it was abruptly hit by collapsing demand for its encryption software products and began burning precious cash. Baltimore's problems were tied to its core software products, based on an encryption technology, Public Key Infrastructure (PKI), which provided 80 per cent of revenues. With economic cutbacks, customers questioned the value of PKI systems. When Microsoft released Windows 2000 bundling in a free version of PKI, the effect was disastrous because Baltimore relied heavily on revenues from this core product: customers had no need to purchase PKI from Baltimore if they received it free with the newly updated Microsoft operating system. Microsoft became notorious during the late 1990s for 'bundling' other innovative applications in with its operating systems as a way of destroying its competitors. The effect on Baltimore was shattering. When interim results were announced in August 2001, it had already issued three profit warnings within a year of having lost its chief executive, founder Fran Rooney, who resigned in May. Restructuring became inevitable.

At a high of 1,375p in spring 2000 the company briefly entered the FTSE 100, but the share price began a steep decline; on the release of these grim interim figures it hit 22.5p. Sales fell from £22.9 million in the first quarter to £16.5 million in the second. Overall losses were £550 million compared to £20 million in August 2000, but the company was valued only at £115 million. The loss per share was a shocking 115p compared to 5.5p for 2000. The overall losses included exceptional items of £389 million on charges linked to the collapse in value of the Content acquisition. The capital markets were averse to new funding and cash from disenchanted shareholders through a rights issue was impossible; inevitably, Baltimore announced it had put its expensive recent acquisition, Content, up for sale, the centrepiece for a massive restructuring. Investors were shocked by this ragged collapse: the forced sale of Content, acquired as recently as the previous autumn for a stunning £692 million, marked an unspoken admission that Baltimore's strategy of rapid acquisitions relying on its previously high share price had failed. Content was expected to raise a mere fraction of its acquisition price, paid seven months earlier. Analysts estimated its sale value at £25 million to £40 million, a disastrous destruction of wealth.

Content Technologies was finally sold for £20.5 million in January 2002, yet when the purchase was arranged, Baltimore thought it would produce substantial cross-selling opportunities. Announcing the proposed sale, interim chief executive Paul Saunders, conceded there were limited synergies between Baltimore Technologies and Content; they were clearly different businesses. 'We did five acquisitions in one year. Companies do tend to focus on acquisitions when the market is going up and can lose focus,' he said. As part of its drastic restructuring, Baltimore planned to delist from the Nasdaq index and reduce its workforce by a third within a year, to secure annual savings of £72 million and restore it to profitability by 2003 without further financing.

Early in October Baltimore announced another boardroom shuffle alongside weak third quarter revenues. The company's value had collapsed from £5.1 billion at the peak to about £82 million. Newly appointed chief executive, Bijan Khezri, formerly a non-executive director of the company, confessed, 'I do not think the board has credibility with the investment community.' But he added, 'The employees, technology and customer base are too good to fail.' At the end of October Bijan Khezri and his fellow directors agreed to drastic pay cuts to conserve dwindling cash, down at £32.4 million; the share price had collapsed 99 per cent from the 2000 peak to a lowly 16.5p.

What a disaster for shareholders hoping for a revival. The situation seemed to lurch from one crisis to another but extensive coverage on various occasions in the financial press charted the stages of its awesome disintegration. The sequence of events reveals how long it took for the crisis to become unmanageable and the speed of the final collapse.

Sequence of events at Baltimore Technologies

1998, December: Zergo takes over Baltimore, a private company for £35 million

2000

January: Baltimore buys US rival CyberTrust, for $150 million in shares

February: Share price peaks at 1,375p

March: Takes a 72.5 per cent stake in its Japanese distributor for £15.8 million

March: Enters the FTSE 100 index

May: Directors sell nearly £12 million of shares. Founder and chief executive, Fran Rooney, resigns

June: Exits FTSE 100 index

September: All-share acquisition of Content Technologies for £692 million

September: Re-enters FTSE 100 index

December: Exits FTSE 100 index

2001

March: First profit warning

April: Second profit warning

June: Third profit warning

August: Content Technologies is put up for sale

Early October: Share price collapses to 16.5p

End October: Bijan Khezri appointed chief executive officer

Source: Based on information in *Financial Times*, 19 October 2001, from Thomson Financial Datastream

Baltimore faces a formidable challenge, but Bijan Khezri was contrite, admitting the company had ignored basic business practices. He set some key objectives: to make the company profitable and show its competence with cash-management. 'This company,' he noted, 'has been paying outrageous salaries. Fran Rooney was paid £450,000. No senior executive, including myself, should be paid more than £150,000.' He confessed that despite the soaring share price in the late 1990s, Baltimore had never produced a profit. 'We need to show we can have a profitable business model. I wonder if we have made any money from any of our transactions. They have not been properly priced.'

Within a fortnight of these remarks Baltimore announced a

round of pay cuts for directors, designed to trim costs and conserve cash. We saw at Independent Insurance how a generous dividend policy favoured directors who were large shareholders. Investors should be mindful of the consequences for careful management when press coverage exposes these types of director excesses.

Baltimore's plan to tackle the major issues that were crippling the group sheds light on what investors should assess if they decide to stay invested in such companies, hoping for an eventual recovery and revival of its fortunes. In Chapter 9, 'Keep Tracking', we look in detail at how investors should evaluate possible recovery prospects for companies like Baltimore that hit dreadful problems (see pp. 158–60).

Misery at Marconi

The speed at which companies unravel when they hit severe problems can be staggeringly fast, as we saw with Independent Insurance and Baltimore Technologies. What happened at Marconi was infinitely worse. Watching the collapse of the UK's flagship technology company was as riveting to seasoned investors as television graphics of a giant star blowing itself to bits in outer space.

Over several decades Lord Arnold Weinstock built a huge electrical manufacturing empire, a solid performer paying a reliable dividend. GEC was a founder member of the elite FTSE 100 index when it was formed in 1984, a British success story while under his control. Lord Weinstock trained a generation of British managers, including Roy Gardner of Centrica and Dr Martin Read of Logica. Sadly, it took only three years for his successors to effectively destroy what he had so frugally assembled. During the 1990s GEC's core businesses were superseded by digital and optic-fibre technology, where it had a smaller presence. Like Nokia, Lord Weinstock favoured cautious joint ventures but this produced a cumbersome corporate structure with numerous partners.

Lord Weinstock chose George Simpson as chief executive to succeed him in 1996. Simpson planned to transform GEC into a fast-track telecommunications infrastructure equipment manufacturer to catapult it into the modern era. The first stage was a £7.7 billion merger for GEC's defence arm with BAE Systems in 1999 plus the name change to Marconi, symbolising its new economy future. Lord Simpson spent all the cash received from this defence sale to BAE Systems plus the entire cash reserves that had been so carefully husbanded over decades by his predecessor, Lord Weinstock. All the money disappeared on a three-year acquisition spree, buying American companies in high technology infrastructure production, where double-digit growth was predicted. Institutional investors were supportive and during the boom few adverse comments emerged.

As any committed shopper knows, an inherited fortune can be quickly spent; Marconi's chief executive supported by its investment bank advisers were not the only well-paid, well-intentioned city experts to be totally beguiled by the high-tech boom. The American acquisitions converted the cash pile into debts of nearly £3 billion by mid-2001. Debts are manageable with expanding revenues but rapidly become a liability in a downturn, as was acutely evident at Baltimore Technologies.

With the collapsing technology bubble Marconi's share price began sliding from its 2000 peak of 1,250p, as American telecoms infrastructure rivals, Lucent Technologies, Canadian Nortel Networks and market leader Cisco Systems were reporting steep declines in demand.

Marconi bought second tier companies, not leaders in their sectors, thereby losing a vital leading edge in any of its chosen product areas. As we saw, a leading edge is imperative if fast-growing companies are to reach ambitious targets. Some critics complained Marconi was operating in too many areas on too small a scale, another weakness of groups who diversify too widely rather than focus on key profitable core businesses. Others argued a lack of global dominance in any of its fields left it weak and vulnerable, reflecting a failure to build niche products or niche markets, another primary goal for successful groups. This contrasted with French Alcatel, a conglomerate that reinvented itself as a telecoms provider through several US acquisitions but emerged as global leader in DSL (digital subscriber lines), the innovative broadband technology destined to feature prominently in expanding Internet usage. Marconi's plight was compounded by a collapse in demand before completing its transformation.

With the growing crisis, one unforgiving fund manager quipped, 'They piled into the tech market at the peak. It's the old adage, if you buy something from the Americans, it's because no other Americans want it.' When the last major purchases were made, the technology sector was peaking. Company directors or private investors who buy at a peak face a guaranteed recipe for capital destruction. British Telecom, a major Marconi client, had publicly announced cutbacks. With orders disappearing trade union officials in Coventry, where Marconi had two of its largest plants, reported to management the declining workloads in April 2001. Lack of work gave workers at the Liverpool Edge Lane factory time to sunbathe, yet management remained unconcerned. Roy Gardner of Centrica repeated essential advice learned from Lord Weinstock when he worked at GEC in the 1970s and 1980s, 'No matter what you do, never lose touch with the detail.' In Gardner's opinion, 'What has happened at Marconi could not have happened under the old GEC management. It's amazing that they [Marconi's directors] did not seem to know what was happening. Either they changed the control environment or totally ignored what they were told.'

Only the paranoid survive

Andy Grove, chairman of Intel

Marconi has a presence [in the growing market for next generation DWDM] but is not at the edge of the innovative curve, nor do they have much market share

Neil Rikard, research director at Gartner

In early July new order figures for the previous quarter presented to the board totally belied their confidence. Realising they would have to announce a profit warning of around 50 per cent on the same day as announcing an asset sale to Philips, an inner group of directors took the unprecedented step of suspending Marconi's shares for a day, almost unheard of for a FTSE 100 giant; investors were left to fret over possible disasters without being able to sell until the shares returned from suspension. Within days, this was seen as a monumental misjudgement, swiftly forcing the 'resignation' of the finance officer. Simpson, discredited by this torrent of adversity, announced a two-month operational review of Marconi's core businesses prior to reorganisation. His position seemed untenable and would be tolerated only until new management could be installed.

What solutions faced Marconi when it announced this profit warning? Its borrowing facilities exceeded £3 billion to tide it through a crisis, but this would incur high additional interest payments. Talk circulated of further asset sales worth around £500 million amid rumours of passing the dividend to conserve another £100 million. Marconi might be forced to raise funds from shareholders to repair the balance sheet but this seemed improbable with a discredited management. Was Marconi a takeover target? Perhaps, but all its close competitors were experiencing the same stark trading conditions and similar problems: declining demand, mounting, unsustainable debts and uncertainty about future orders.

Sinking confidence

While Marconi undertook the two-month operational review, major rival Cisco Systems announced a massive restructuring, indicating the extent of changes Marconi might need. Knowing profit warnings seldom arrive singly, fears of more bad news rocked Marconi's share price during August, although directors insisted the finances were sound. Then, a financial bombshell: with the share price around 75p, an analyst at Goldman Sachs stunned the market by announcing Marconi's shares were worth 55p. Within days the Companies & Markets section of the *Financial Times* set out this valuation.

Marconi sum-of-the-parts valuation

Consolidated division	*Value (£m)*
Communications	3,905
Systems	170
Capital	236
Total	**4,311**
Net debt (2001)	2,966
Market value (balancing figure)	1,345
Stakes in listed companies (added in)	231
Total value	**1,576**
Share value (pence)	57

(based on value divided by number of shares: £1576/2,765 million shares)

Source: *Financial Times*, from Goldman Sachs, 8 August 2001

> *In a time of crisis you can't manage by manual;*
> *you have to manage by values and beliefs*
>
> Kenneth Chenault, chief executive, American Express

Decline and fall

On this devastating analysis Marconi's shares collapsed to 65p; valued at £1,797 million Marconi faced eviction from the FTSE 100 index at September's review. Eviction would force tracker funds to sell their holdings, putting yet more pressure on its sinking value. By 31 August a profit warning from close rival Spirent sent the shares down to 53p. When Marconi's first profit warning shocked the markets on 4 July driving the price down to 112p, shareholders might have thought it too late to sell, as the worst was probably known. Yet within two months, further traumas decimated Marconi to an unimaginable extent. Sometimes, selling at a large loss can avert greater capital destruction. Once again, I return to the lesson I learned by my hasty sale of Polly Peck, described in Chapter 1. A loss of one quarter of my funds was large, but at least I had rescued 75 per cent to reinvest in another company: investors who chose to support Polly Peck until it was suspended lost 100 per cent of their funds.

At its September 2000 peak, Marconi was worth £34.5 billion. When trading resumed on 5 July it was worth £3.1 billion, less than 10 per cent of its value ten months earlier, a stark reverse ten-bagger, trading at levels last seen in the early 1980s. With the second more damaging profit warning, issued on 4 September, accompanied by the forced resignation of Lord Simpson and Sir Roger Hurn, chairman, the shares plunged on worries over monumental debts and survival prospects. The first quarter loss and higher than expected debts led to incredible activity and wild share price swings, ending the day at 53p on huge volume of 140 million shares traded. On 5 September extensive press coverage of Marconi's plight was intensified by cautious statements from rivals Ericsson and Motorola, and a warning from Alcatel about challenging market conditions. Further sharp broker downgrades unsettled investors, sending the shares along their astonishing descent to a twenty-three-year record low of 38p, not seen since the 1970s, on huge volume of 172 million shares traded.

Analysts said investors were valuing Marconi as if it faced bankruptcy, but Adrian Murray at Teather & Greenwood's switched his recommendation from 'sell' to 'strong buy' as Marconi's trading statement allayed his fears of a rights issue: 'People just don't believe the company. People are basically saying that the company's going bust. We're just going to have to wait and see.' He expected Marconi to trade out of its present plight, but this made some heroic assumptions, including a rapid recovery in demand for optical network equipment; most brokers were more negative. In his influential column, Barry Riley summarised Marconi's dilemma:

> *Within the last two years it [Marconi] has spent $7 billion on what had proved to be almost worthless Internet equipment companies. The scale of value destruction had been truly spectacular, and arguably without rational explanation: in twelve months Marconi's shareholders had suffered a loss in value of £33.7 billion.*
>
> Barry Riley, 'The Long View', *Financial Times*, 8 September 2001

On 6 September the shares suffered a further savage assault, in an unrelenting selling blitz, shedding 23 per cent to close at 29p on the heaviest volume yet, 214.4 million shares traded; with Marconi valued at a lowly £807 million, it recorded one of the worst decimations in modern UK corporate history. It is tempting to write history backwards, but during 1999 and early 2000, as acquisitions converted Marconi into a telecoms infrastructure manufacturer, brokers, analysts and institutional investors were supportive. The list revealing broker optimism, published by the *Financial Times* in mid-September 2001 looked hopelessly misjudged. But rampant over-optimism had been wide-ranging; it engulfed over 90 per cent of experts, investors and company bosses at the time.

List of broker recommendations and share prices on Marconi

1999

17 December: Charles Stanley, 'buy' at 953p

2000

26 July: UBS Warburg, 'buy' at 1070p

September: Underwriters to Marconi's £1.8 billion convertible bond include Morgan Stanley Dean Witter (MSDW), Credit Suisse First Boston (CSFB), JP Morgan, Merrill Lynch, Schroder Salomon Smith Barney and UBS Warburg

14 September: Deutsche Bank, 'market perform' at 1049p

6 December: ABN Amro, 'add' at 735p

2001

11 April: (MSDW), 'outperform' at 341p

15 May: Commerzbank advises 'hold' at 358p

9 July: Nomura, 'hold' at 110p

Source: *Financial Times*, 11 September 2001, p. 26

With the shares at 38p, Robert Cole in *The Times* Business section questioned Marconi's recovery projections following Alcatel's gloomy forecasts and pessimistic talk from Ericsson and Motorola. If demand remained depressed for telecoms infrastructure equipment, Marconi would have difficulty generating £500 million of operating cash flow required to balance the sums. Debt of £4.4 billion was targeted to fall to £3.2 billion by March 2002, requiring more asset sales; restructuring required £450 million plus £170 million for interest payments. Recovery hinged on the £500 million of positive operating cash flow Marconi predicted. Yet first half cash flow had been negative, with £533 million lost. Facing low demand, a similar sum might be lost in the second half. Without that £500 million contribution debts would stay high, perhaps leading to the bankruptcy the share price indicated. Large asset disposals jeopardise future profitability, so he advised, 'Things could still get worse. Sell.'

Press reports revealed banks were demanding higher interest rates on Marconi's debts; the company's bonds were relegated to 'junk' (virtually worthless) status by credit rating agency, Standard & Poor's, swiftly followed by Moody's. Richard Windsor, analyst at Nomura, thought the severity of the collapse was another factor jeopardising Marconi's survival: 'Looking at this share price you are now looking at a market expectation that this company is going bankrupt. The real danger is that people like BT will take one look at the share price and start buying their equipment elsewhere, and if that happens there's a big problem.'

The horrific September 2001 terrorist attacks on America brought further downward spirals for most equities; Marconi's shares lost another 31 per cent, to 17p, 98 per cent below their peak, valuing the group at £473 million. Marconi's ten-year euro-denominated bonds fell below 30 per cent of their face value. Williams de Broé told clients, 'In all probability the shares are worthless, but this will not become apparent for some time.'

One positive result was a warning from the Financial Services Authority (FSA) about keeping shareholders fully informed: 109 trading statements, including several profit warnings were issued in the five weeks from 3 September to 6 October 2001 compared with thirty-seven in the corresponding period of 2000.

When Marconi issued an update trading statement in January 2002, hopes for a swift turnround faded. The group reported poor sales and increased losses for its third quarter and expressed pessimism about short-term improvements. As further asset disposals occurred, analysts doubted whether the remaining divisions could achieve adequate profitability to vouchsafe the company's future suvival. During spring 2002 Marconi's creditors were negotiating a debt-for-equity swap, which would substantially dilute shareholders' equity. Marconi owed £4 billion to its banks and bondholders.

Events in Marconi's Crisis

1996, September: Lord Simpson becomes chief executive

1999

January: GEC sells defence business to BAE Systems

March: GEC buys Reltec for £1.3 billion

April: Fore Systems purchased for £2.6 billion

June: Name changed to Marconi

2001

April: Shares trade around 310p. Credit Suisse First Boston rates them a 'buy'

16 April: Major rival Cisco Systems issues a profit warning, sacking 25 per cent of its workforce

May: Reports a pre-tax loss of £61 million for the year to 31 March 2001, down from profits of £523 million for 2000

17 May: Lord Simpson predicts recovery in telecoms market in the second half of the year and predicts full-year profits rise for Marconi

June: Shares trade around 268p. UBS Warburg rates them a 'buy'

15 June: Canadian rival Nortel Networks warns of second quarter $19 billion loss

3 July: Unprecedented one-day full suspension announced after market closed with Marconi's shares at 264p

4 July: At 6.53 p.m., the first profit warning is announced: full-year profits estimated to halve. Another 4,000 jobs are cut

5 July: Shares resume trading at 112.5p

6 July: John Mayo, chief executive-designate, forced to resign. Lord Simpson and Sir Roger Hurn remain

18 July: Marconi faces down shareholder revolt at Annual General Meeting. Lord Simpson announces a two-month strategic review and pledges to shareholders, 'If anything changes we commit to coming back to you with an update.' He reassures shareholders on Marconi's prospects

20 August: Lord Simpson takes a two-week holiday. The shares trade around 75p

30 August: Marconi assures the union there will be no more job losses and agrees to further meetings

1 September: BT, Marconi's biggest customer, pledges £10 billion in cost savings

4 September: Lord Simpson and Sir Roger Hurn are forced to resign as Marconi cuts another 2,000 jobs and reveals a first quarter loss of £227 million and up to £4.15 million in provisions. The shares close down at 53p on massive volume of 140 million shares traded

5 September: Another shocking plunge of 28 per cent takes the share price down to 38p as brokers and investors assess Marconi's survival prospects

6 September: Shares plunge another 23.7 per cent, to 29p on massive volume of 214.4 million shares traded, valuing the company at just £807 million

12 September: Marconi, a founder member of the FTSE 100 index in 1984, is evicted from the list of top 100 companies

21 September: Shares collapse to 20p on volume of 89.6 million shares traded, valuing it at £556.6 million on a day of panic on global stock markets, reflecting the market's view that the deteriorating global situation threatens bankruptcy for heavily indebted firms

27 September: Shares collapse by another 31 per cent to 17p on heavy volume of 170 million shares traded on pessimistic broker views

2 October: Shares trade at 14p, valuing Marconi at a lowly £375 million

9 October: Marconi appoints new lead financial adviser, Lazard, and new broker, Cazenove

10 October: After much adverse press comment, Lord Simpson agrees to accept a smaller final compensation package of £1.5 million for his loss of office, below his contractual compensation but provoking outrage among workers, shareholders and the press

15 October: Marconi announces second quarter results in line with previous guidance, while net debt was 'below £4.3 billion'. The share price rises to 44p on the trading statement, perhaps in relief. But the company remains in 'intensive care'

2002

15 January: In a trading statement Marconi says it does not expect to see any improvement in its trading situation for the whole of 2002

March: Marconi unveils a record £5.7 billion loss for its last financial year

Having charted this stunning collapse, we can briefly note the factors that destroyed the three companies we have examined: Independent Insurance, Baltimore Technologies and Marconi.

> *Ambitious targets are fine, but not at the expense of losing the plot*
>
> Fergus O'Connell, author of books on high-tech projects

Identity pointers to the losing profiles of Independent Insurance, Baltimore Technologies and Marconi

Unfocused or misguided management with a weak business plan
When Assessors Watson Wyatt discovered previously undisclosed liabilities at Independent Insurance the implication was that either there had been deliberate concealment or perhaps poor attention to daily procedures. At Baltimore, interim chief executive Paul Saunders implied a loss of focus when the company embarked on an acquisition plan, making five acquisitions in one year. We saw how inattentive Marconi's management were to profit warnings reported by major US rivals and to employee cautions over dwindling workloads. It was evident tight control systems were no longer in place, a detrimental change from Lord Weinstock's regime.

Operates in a mature market with low future growth potential
Insurance is a centuries-old industry in Britain, but investors

thought Independent had found a profitable niche to exploit. Baltimore's niche within fast-growing security software ultimately proved a weakness when Microsoft destroyed their marketing push; while Marconi's restructuring coincided with massive over-investment in the telecoms infrastructure market, jeopardising its growth plans.

Crowded market with low entry costs and too many competitors In the UK, insurance is an overcrowded market while we have seen how competition from Microsoft damaged Baltimore's revenue prospects. Marconi's strategy seemed sensible but massive injections of venture capital funds lowered the cost of entry to the industry, generating a broadband glut.

Few opportunities to become a leading edge company This failing applied to all three companies. Lacking global dominance in any of its chosen fields, Marconi, critics argued, was vulnerable in a downturn.

May not be highly cash generative and may embark on a rapid expansion programme A rapid, misguided acquisition policy hit the performance of both Baltimore Technologies and Marconi, bringing virtual ruin to them both. Inattention to the costs of new acquisitions turned cash-rich GEC into debt-laden Marconi within three years.

Mounting debts This was a feature that initiated horrendous problems for all three companies. In September 2001 Marconi's debts were £4.3 billion, targeted to fall to £3.2 billion by March 2002; valued at only £800 million, its survival was threatened.

Misuse of the brand advantage, associated with adverse publicity when the company is forced to cope in public with its problems We saw in each case how adverse publicity to the emergence of financial problems hit the share price. Assessors at Independent Insurance discovered 'previously undisclosed liabilities'. The resignation of founder Fran Rooney knocked investor confidence at Baltimore, while for Marconi, in particular, extensive press comment about its uncertain survival led to mounting concern that its heavily publicised problems might deter new orders.

Shrinking market share, numbers of clients or contracts Shrinking market share and nervous clients became part of Baltimore's and Marconi's high profile collapses.

Diversifying into new products or markets instead of focusing on the core business This failing was a contributory problem at all three companies, while critics thought Marconi operated in too many product areas on too small a scale.

May hit a crisis due to poor management decisions and high debts In all three cases, an acute crisis emerged as a result of poor management decisions and mounting debts. In particular, Marconi's collapse was an appalling demonstration of a crisis-strewn scenario.

Learning how to lose

Marconi's tragedy makes sobering reading for investors hoping to profit from backing great British or foreign-based companies. Fortunately such a catastrophe is rare. Concerned investors holding shares in suspect companies should follow professional analysis in the financial press to aid decision-making. You do not need to be an accountant to compute for yourself whether a failing company can survive, but reading crucial analysis by brokers or financial journalists is essential: in Marconi's case, financial press coverage highlighted the complete story. You do not need to know if broker assessments are accurate or not: your one concern is to decide whether you will continue supporting current management. This is the enduring value of updating yourself about companies you own or plan to own shares in.

Investors must consider if recovery looks realistic within a reasonable time frame. Are prospects based on over-optimistic forecasts? The three architects of Marconi's conversion and subsequent rout were out of touch with daily operational activities. Lord Simpson claimed he could hand over the reins to his deputy and 'take off his working shoes' for several months while his successor worked his way into the job. However, as we saw, winning companies have visionary bosses with a workaholic attitude to their businesses. When rival companies report sombre news investors should suspect that problems might arise in their company even if management insist everything is fine.

In summer 2001, with share prices plunging, it was difficult to decide which were more depressed – prices or investors. Yet even amid the wreckage, glimpses of survival tactics were emerging. The severity of the bear market dissipated enthusiasm for weak business plans, forcing companies to face the reality that the best share price drivers are rising revenues and profits, ideas temporarily ignored during the boom.

You can't hit a home run on a soft ball

Ronald Reagan, fortieth President of the United States

4 Tilting the Odds

An investment is simply a gamble in which you have managed to tilt the odds in your favour

Peter Lynch, manager of Fidelity's Magellan Fund, 1977–90

When I was making the *Mrs Cohen's Money* television series, I met a man who said he regularly read my column in the *Mail on Sunday*. Thinking he was reading it for investment ideas, I asked if he was an investor but he said, 'No, I follow the horses.' Did he, I asked, make money from betting? To which he admitted he sometimes did. If you want to make money from a serious hobby, investing or backing horses, you need a good system and the discipline to follow it. Fail to observe these two essentials and your chances of becoming a loser increase alarmingly: the bookies or the market exploit your weaknesses and simply pocket your cash. Backing winners is the only sensible route to profitable investment, but famous generals know the importance of tilting the odds. One of Napoleon's great military maxims was, 'When you determine to risk a battle, reserve to yourself every possible chance of success': focus on threats and the possibilities of failure and devise contingency plans.

Following a system has much to recommend it, as you are ready to cope if problems arise when events throw schemes into short-term disarray. If the market collapses, will it catch you unprepared? Do you have a back-up plan to tackle that eventuality? Do you know now what you would do if a company whose shares you hold issues a profit warning or sacks its chief executive? Even when there are no sudden alarms, these decisions are better planned for in advance: pre-planning for setbacks is a valuable way to tilt the odds towards winning.

Recognising the symptoms of failure

The millennium boom fallout was so immense it produced an enormous collection of losers. This proved an excellent time to write about distinguishing between winning and losing business strategies, but it was a sorry time for investors, including me, caught up in these multiple corporate disasters.

In Chapter 3 we saw how to recognise early warnings in failing companies. As with diagnosing a disease, there can be several relevant symptoms but not every patient has all of them. A smart doctor can make a sound diagnosis on the basis of probabilities. The more symptoms that point to one disease, the more certain he can be about his judgement. A cluster of symptoms adds to his growing certainty that he knows what ails the patient. From there, it is a short step to deciding on appropriate treatment. And so it is with failing companies. Even if not all the defining symptoms are present, in most cases the warning signs are sufficiently common to compile the average profile of failure. Knowing this profile gives investors a huge advantage over those who are unaware of this formula, because investors gain confidence to act promptly when some of these important warning signs appear in companies they own shares in. Following the formula enables investors to make earlier, more confident selling decisions. Knowing when to sell and let go of losing investments is one of the hardest investment tests. But as it is among the major routes to successful results, it is vital to learn this skill as early as possible, even if selling involves a large and painful loss.

If you say you never had a chance, perhaps you never took a chance
Howard Schultz, founder of Starbucks Corporation, the coffee shop chain

Learn from others

We can put some figures on the idea that frequent trading damages a portfolio's value. Every purchase entails commission, stamp duty and the spread between the buying and selling prices quoted by market makers. Costs are disproportionately larger for sums below £500. Investing £100 costs commission of £15 plus stamp duty and the market maker's spread (the difference between the buying and selling prices quoted). For some shares where daily volumes traded are modest, the market maker's spread will be 5p or 10p, but for a share such as Vodafone where volumes traded frequently exceed 300 million a day, the spread can be very small, say 179.5p to sell and 180p to buy. But even with this small spread, your share must rise nearly 20 per cent before you start to see profit, an immediate hurdle, shown in the example below. However, this is only half the story, because when you sell, another £15 commission is payable. Therefore, when spending only £100 to buy shares, the price must rise above 36 per cent to cover the total costs. This still leaves you all square without showing a gain.

Example I

Costs incurred when buying Vodafone shares for £500

Purchase of 268 Vodafone shares at 180p (268 × 180p)	£482.40
Stamp duty of 0.5% (£482.40 × 0.05)	£2.41
Commission to broker	£15
Total cost	**£499.81**
Average cost per share (£499.81 ÷ 268)	186.5p
Selling commission to broker	£15
Selling price required to break even	192p (6.7%)

Example II

Costs incurred when buying Vodafone shares for £100

Purchase of 47 Vodafone shares at 180p	£84.60
Stamp duty of 0.5% (£84.60 × 0.05)	£0.42
Commission to broker	£15
Total cost	£100.02
Average cost per share (£100.02 ÷ 47)	2.13p
Selling price required to break even	214p (18.9%)
Selling price to break even after commission	245p (36.1%)

As frequent trading racks up costs, it is counterproductive for investors hoping to double their money, and hampers the goal for tenfold rises. Even if you take a longer-term view than day traders, it helps to know the most common mistakes novice investors make to further tilt the odds towards success by avoiding them in future. All mistakes are detrimental to wealth creation but all these common errors involve high risks. Surprisingly, most novice investors follow a similar route and repeat these common mistakes.

The ultimate risk is not taking a risk

Sir James Goldsmith, financier and entrepreneur

The ten most common investor mistakes

1 *They expect to make quick profits* without doing any homework or detective work on fundamental information about shares before they buy. In the late 1990s amateurs treated the stock market like a casino with easy money on offer. Beginner's luck can work but all too frequently dreams of quick profits turn into the nightmares of rapid losses.

2 *They tend to invest heavily when the market is highly valued.* During the 2001 slowdown, investors showed signs of contrary behaviour. Instead of buying for the long term most had completely lost interest in the market. Figures from Autif

(Association of Unit and Investment Trusts) showed that gross retail sales fell almost 16 per cent in July 2001, compared to July 2000. This decline followed an 'Isa season' (Individual Savings Accounts) from January to 5 April, in which investors had shunned the market as prices fell. The previous year had been a bumper 'Isa season' with heavy buying. As markets boomed towards their spring peaks, investors poured cash into high technology funds.

Such figures underline the bald facts: private investors buy shares when they are relatively expensive but shun them when they are cheaper. Buying at high prices inevitably brings losses which is discouraging. Predicting a market low is impossible but as prices fall a sensible strategy of steady buying in modest amounts puts your cash into the market ready for gains as recovery begins. Buying late is a sure route to capital destruction.

Anyway, most private investors are natural trend-chasers, who pile in near bull market peaks, rather than 'bottom fishers' who can cope with the gloom and alarm typical of bear market lows

Barry Riley, *FT Money*, 15 September 2001

In *The Bear Book*,* John Rothchild notes a retired US investor who bought shares months before the October 1929 crash probably died before breaking even. A forty-year-old buying long term in early 1929 would not have seen a whiff of profit until he retired in 1954. This, however, is a jaundiced view. Anyone unlucky enough to be sucked into equities near a market peak must revise the strategy to tilt the odds back towards winning. Investors who bought dear should regard the setback as a pothole along the route to wealth creation, not a permanent roadblock. Continue saving regularly, as described in Chapter 5. At the age of forty there is plenty of time to rectify a poor

*John Rothchild, *The Bear Book*, John Wiley & Sons, 1998.

financial situation before retirement looms. I was fifty-three when I fell hopelessly into debt; by my early sixties the family's fortunes were completely transformed: a constructive rescue plan based on your own efforts makes the difference. Confront a bad situation, set new targets, adopt the Ten-point Action Plan, and you are ready to invest your way out of debt and losses.

Do not undermine your efforts for massive returns by ignoring the market, as you might be tempted to buy when others are buying, most often when prices are too high. We know the market is nearer to a peak than a trough when widespread TV news or newspaper coverage reports it is hitting new highs.

Having been investing for twelve years, I have watched three downturns, two of which led on to recession; the 1991–2 recession was among the worst since 1945; the 1994–5 recession saw bonds record their worst year for decades; finally 1998 turned out to be a swift plunge in share prices followed by a rapid recovery. I have used these occasions to reshuffle my portfolio. During periods of deep investor gloom selling can be timely if proceeds are reinvested at relatively low prices in better opportunities, ready for the next upturn. Forget the get-rich-quick formulas, do some detective work to find the profitable opportunities and watch your profits grow during the next bull market. Buying cautiously on down days over several months at low prices has a proven track record. Indeed, what works for companies should work for investors: companies that fared best during the 1980s and 1990s were those such as Intel that kept investing right through the downturns.

3 *They take tips from newspapers, friends or tip sheets without doing any homework.* This exposes investors to higher risks than necessary since very few UK companies will become big winners. When a newsletter tips a share, the market makers raise the price immediately, putting buyers at a disadvantage. Stock picking for sound prospects cannot rely on tips, but they might be a suitable starting point for research, so are not to be dismissed completely.

Every time you 'get it wrong', you increase the odds to 'get it right'
Richard Wilkins, author of inspirational books

4 *They may put too much cash into just one or two investments*, a high-risk approach. Everyone needs a well-balanced portfolio of assets, but figures consistently show that too many adults in Britain hold most of their funds in deposit savings accounts, where interest rates are meagre when inflation is low, although the capital can still lose its purchasing power even with inflation as low as 2 per cent. The capital will lose half its purchasing power in thirty-five years with inflation at 2 per cent.

Recent statistics revealed that some savers in Equitable Life, the failing insurance company had three, four or even more policies with just this one company, exposing them to very high risks when its major problems on honouring its annuity guarantees emerged.

5 *They adopt a high-risk approach to direct shareholdings*, by focusing on just one or two often with household names. Many investors have fallen into the trap of not building a balanced portfolio by acquiring privatisation or former building society-turned-bank shares including major groups such as Abbey National, Halifax Bank or Alliance & Leicester. If they hold two shares and by some unfortunate chance both companies hit trouble, the portfolio offers no offsetting protection. During the late 1990s three of the UK's most popular shares – BT, Marks & Spencer and J. Sainsbury – dramatically lost direction; over 250,000 shareholders in Railtrack plus 12,000 employees were left holding worthless shares when it was unexpectedly put into administration on 5 October 2001, although the government subsequently agreed to pay some compensation to investors.

6 *They buy or sell shares on short-term price fluctuations*, which is a poor guide for investment decisions. Avoid this losing strategy by following the Ten-point Action Plan. Set realistic long-term growth targets and think like a long-term investor to ride out short-term

gyrations. However, be ready to reassess a shareholding when a company hits a rough patch. Volume figures show the heaviest selling occurs at market lows. The largest numbers of sellers appear at the time of maximum loss in a falling market. In America shares hit savage lows on huge volumes in 1929, 1937, 1974 and as recently as 21 September 2001. With prices spiralling down, investors hesitate until, in a general panic, they finally act. Smart investors use the opposite strategy: buying when prices are lower and markets are depressed. Although many investors, including me, find it difficult to decide when to buy shares in falling markets; advice to buy low sounds excellent in theory but is difficult to practise. Another, equally effective route, which I often follow, is buying small blocks of shares and adding more if prices fall below the price I originally paid. This worked well with my purchases of Royal Bank of Scotland and again with ARM Holdings. In late June 2001 I bought a small holding of ARM at 242p but on 21 September 2001, when a major panic hit international stock markets, I was able to buy a much larger holding at 197p, to bring the average cost of the total holding down to 220p. In March 2001 I bought half my intended holding of Royal Bank of Scotland at 1,489p only to see the price plunge the very next day. By waiting a few more days I was able to pick up the second half of my holding for 1,339p, which brought the average cost of the total holding down to 1,433p.

7 *They take small profits* rather than allow successful shares to fulfil their long-term potential. By seeking out profitable ten-bagger prospects and following the Ten-point Action Plan investors will avoid this frustrating mistake.

8 *They hold losing shares for too long*, hoping for an ultimate recovery, to sell without taking a loss. Waiting for recovery in a losing share is an act of faith, not a sound strategy; the exact opposite to sensible action: far better to sell losers fast and run winners longer. A disciplined approach to eliminating losers avoids

this self-defeating error. Knowing which features identify ten-baggers reduces the chances of buying shares with low prospects.

9 *They follow investment fads and fashions*, instead of choosing sound long-term investment opportunities. Fashions can abruptly become hot topics but just as rapidly lose their popularity. Following fashions seems harmless but can prove expensive, as anyone who became a quoted football club investor in the late 1990s knows.

Attitude is a magic word in every language

Kemmons Wilson, hotelier and founder of Holiday Inns, hotel chain

In February 1997 stockbroker Nomura started tracking the twelve listed football clubs, with a corny 'footie' index. That January investment bank Singer & Friedlander had launched a football fund, attracting over £36 million. The float of new funds in a promising sector often occurs as a market peaks when the sector is attracting most press coverage and investor interest. Manchester City and Tottenham Hotspur had floated in the 1980s; by January 1997 both were showing huge rises, up from 210p in late 1995 to around 700p. Several other clubs had floated over the previous few months while more were preparing to float that spring. The whole sector buzzed with promise, on the pitch and the stock market. With so much hype the sector looked ripe for profit taking. It seemed exciting for football fans to discover they could follow their teams on the field and make profits from their football hobby on the stock market. Amid this euphoria, I was cautious, as I wrote in my diary for the *Mail on Sunday* that March. A major accounting firm had just issued a report rating the quoted clubs collectively overvalued by around £1 billion.

By 2001 exuberance had evaporated. When Manchester United announced a 30 per cent leap in pre-tax profits up from

£16.8 million in 2000 to £21.8 million for 2001, investors seemed unimpressed; they disregarded the good news and the share price slid to 125p, little more than half its January 2001 value of 235p and well down from the 2000 peak of 413p. Other club prices were also languishing. All, except Manchester United, seemed financially weak. So what went wrong? Some industries, including technology and telecommunications had deep problems in 2001. The football club problem had much in common with the dotcoms; companies failed to find a workable business model to generate regular profits. Wages and player costs, including vast transfer fees, grew faster than income and gate receipts. Over half the turnover went in wages. This was not a sound formula for running profitable businesses.

Fashion fades – style is eternal

Yves Saint Laurent, fashion designer

10 *They follow experts' advice*, although most mis-selling scandals involved professionals who misled clients, however innocently, by selling them inappropriate or even faulty financial products, as vividly exemplified by one million Equitable Life policyholders. This is a huge dilemma for British investors who have been mis-sold pensions, endowment policies, even annuities, and illustrates the importance of everyone making their own financial decisions. Welcome advice, but be sure you are the person taking the big decisions.

It is YOUR money you are putting at risk.

Great opportunities occur every year in America. Get yourself prepared and go for it. You will find that little acorns can grow into giant oaks

William O'Neil, author of *How to Make Money in Stocks*

Remarkably, many investors, including me, repeat some mistakes many times before finally discarding an unhelpful routine. Eventually, however, even the dumbest of us learns. I recall once being so mad at myself I attached a note to the clipboard of papers I used for trading references. Whenever I lifted the phone to trade, I saw this message: 'This was my last dumb trade.' Today, my self-help message is equally simple: 'Keep backing winners.' But unsurprisingly, that takes time, some effort and plenty of patience.

Where there is a panic, there is also opportunity

John Neff, author of *John Neff on Investing*. John Neff with S. L. Mintz

5 **Design Your Own Portfolio**

And the reward is there for the taking; the only question is: Are you conscious enough to take it?

Bill Williams, *Trading Chaos*

Avoiding risky strategies is crucial to investment success. Interestingly, *The Coming Internet Depression*,* by Michael Mandel, reveals how venture capitalists hedge their bets, using focused ways to weed out losers. They fund plenty of projects, some scarcely more than wild experiments, relying on diversification for capital protection. Backing many companies increases the chance of uncovering an exceptional winner. Cash is spent in stages, cautiously for reassessing the odds of success as projects progress. They stay focused without getting too heavily involved in one project. By refraining to increase their stakes in losing bets, they can fund many more ideas, making much better use of resources to help other start-ups. Ten-bagger hunters can employ similar strategies: spread the risks of backing too many losers by building a balanced portfolio, as we will now discuss.

Portfolio design

The FTSE 100 index appeared to have gone nowhere over the four years from the panic collapse in October 1998 to June 2002: having risen from 4,500 to almost 7,000 by year-end 1999, it then gradually declined back to 4,900 by June 2002. However, not all shares were

*Michael Mandel, *The Coming Internet Depression*, Basic Books, 2000.

back where they started four years earlier: Sage Group was up at around 165p, 65p higher than in the dark days of October 1998; Royal Bank of Scotland was at 1985p from 700p, a rise of 183.5 per cent; SmithKline Beecham had traded at 745p in October 1998 and reached 950p at the time of its merger with Glaxo Wellcome in December 2000, a rise of 27.5 per cent; Perpetual stood at 2,750p in October 1998 and was bought by Amvescap at 3,697p per share in December 2000, a rise of 34 per cent. Knowing that some shares can rise from a trough to record a substantial gain even when the FTSE 100 goes nowhere illustrates the need to back winners. Who said stock picking does not work? However, four years is not a long enough period to leave money in the market: a five-to-ten-year view is the minimum for planning to grow a capital sum.

Stay on track

Every investor should assess the anticipated outcome from holding long-term assets. A FTSE All-Share index tracker fund is a useful balancing foil for the higher-risk ten-bagger portfolio. The tracker aims to match the performance of 750 of the UK's largest companies, spreading your cash widely to reduce risk. Among the 750 will be several small companies to produce a broad cross-section. The tracker fund simply tracks a weighted selection of these companies, falling as they fall and rising when they rise. The tracker will not grow faster than the market nor will it fall further during a downturn. Knowing this eliminates one of the worst aspects of investing – the uncertainty of what to expect.

John C. Bogle, founder of the world's first index-tracker fund Vanguard, is critical of active fund management practices. He launched his first index fund on 30 August 1976 with just $11 million in investments: it is now the world's biggest with assets of $95 billion (£65 billion). He is scornful of the vast US mutual trust (collective funds) industry, especially the recent practice of

100 per cent turnover in equities in actively managed portfolios. In a *Financial Times* interview he said when he started investing in the 1960s the average stock portfolio turnover was 15 per cent, meaning the average stock was held for seven years. Today funds hold equities for an average of one year, arousing cynicism; 'Someone has got to prove to me that that's not short-term speculation.' A twenty-six-year study by the Dalbar rankings agency found that from 1884 to 2000 the average stock fund investor earned only 5.3 per cent a year, although the US S&P 500 index returned 16.29 per cent.

Mutual funds can make no claim to superiority over the market average

John C. Bogle, founder of the Vanguard index-tracker fund

Trackers are organised to back the winners: as shares are demoted or fall out of favour and leave a benchmark index, trackers must sell and buy the new replacement entrants. This gives the tracker an advantage over active funds that may remain invested in demoted companies. Active funds charge higher fees, eating into future profits. However, trackers produce widely varying performances; some charge more than others, some have higher tracking errors, deviating markedly from their benchmark. As trackers are increasingly popular, the financial press covers the sector regularly, reporting on independent surveys highlighting the best and worst funds for readers. In autumn 2001 a survey by Chartwell Investment Management, a Bath-based independent financial adviser, noted high-charging funds for Alliance & Leicester, Bank of Scotland and St James's Place. A tracking error was a consistent feature of all the funds they researched; almost all trackers underperform their benchmarks, specially among FTSE All-Share trackers, as few invest in all 750 companies: most select a representative collection. The research named two All-Share trackers with both low charges and index deviation: M&G All-Share tracker and Prudential. They may change their charging and selection profiles, so investors must stay vigilant for future performance.

Designing the Ten-bagger portfolio

After setting up the FTSE All-Share tracker as a counterweight, designing the ten-bagger portfolio is the next step. How many shares should it hold? How many sectors and which particular ones should be included? How much money should be allocated to each choice?

Careful portfolio design is much neglected but it can spell the difference between outstanding success and mediocrity. Your results could reflect the strengths or weaknesses of the design. Tilt the odds towards winning with a design that maximises the chance of success. This is essential for investors intent on setting up the ten-bagger portfolio as the focal point of their Ten-point Action Plan, and leaving it to run without much supervision. It might take as long as ten to twelve months to find ten suitable candidates that can safely be left to grow without regular reviews of their progress. Selecting your most promising top ten candidates and taking time to buy them at low prices will get your portfolio off to a flying start.

Decide at the outset how large your portfolio will be, based on the total value of your assets. Can you afford £10,000 or would £5,000 initially be more cautious? Even if you have more than £10,000 to invest, it makes sense to start modestly and decide after a year whether following a ten-bagger portfolio suits your investment personality. If you are happy with your progress, topping up the holdings of your favourite ten-baggers is easy, or you might add a few different companies in some new sectors. Have a cut-off point of a maximum fifteen companies, as tracking more is difficult. Start compiling your list of candidates, restricting the total to about twenty. Arrange the selections under their relevant sectors.

There are many different kinds of heroism, and one of them is the quiet heroism of working hard, supporting a family and pursuing a dream

Rudolph Giuliani, New York Mayor, 1 October 2001

Steps for Portfolio Design

1. Decide how large your ten-bagger portfolio will be with a minimum of £5,000 and either ten, twelve or fifteen companies
2. Watch the market over several months to find prospects
3. Compile your preliminary short-list of twenty possible candidates
4. Arrange the choices under separate sectors
5. Whittle these down, retaining seven or eight sectors in the final portfolio
6. When the top ten prospects emerge, arrange a buying plan with target prices to act upon over the following months
7. Begin buying your top prospects
8. After about one year, decide if you want to increase the portfolio size
9. If so, add extra shares to the holdings of your favourite future ten-baggers
10. Or, add up to another five companies for a maximum fifteen companies in total

A spread of sectors

The initial ten-bagger portfolio should hold about seven or eight different sectors. The market covers numerous sectors, although the high-growth areas mainly occur in the information technology, media or telecoms sectors. Information technology is a widely used term; in electronics, information covers anything that can be digitised – encoded as a stream of bits – while technology refers to the infrastructure that makes it possible to store, search, retrieve, copy, manipulate, view, transmit and receive information. Information technology covers many sectors: information technology hardware, software and computer services, support systems and some distributors. New entrants have emerged in the telecoms, biotechnology and drug start-ups. The general retailers group includes some popular discount retailers; several fast-growing firms are in oil exploration, mining and property, small fund managers and other speciality finance providers. As you design your portfolio, keep the selections under their appropriate sectors, honing them down while trying to retain at least seven or eight sectors. When the top ten prospects emerge, arranged by sectors, work out a buying plan to include target buy prices, procedures we will cover in Chapter 8.

We know indexing always wins and wins massively
John C. Bogle, founder of the Vanguard index-tracker fund

A balanced portfolio

One unmistakable sign that markets are nearing a peak is when figures reveal that novice investors become active, often as vigorous day traders. Repeatedly, evidence shows amateur investors who do not usually follow the market are keen buyers as they see the market rising. Because novices tend to act in large numbers when a top is near, long-term investors can use this as a signal that markets might soon fall, offering buying opportunities at lower prices.

The start of a new tax year is a good time to allocate cash for a tax-friendly Maxi Isa to invest around £580 each month into a unit or investment trust FTSE All-Share tracker, as a balance for the higher risk ten-bagger portfolio. An alternative would be to use the Isa allocation for building your ten-bagger portfolio; buy four or five shares in several blocks of around £1,000 over about six months to a year, in a self-select Maxi Isa where you choose the shares yourself. Start with large UK FTSE 100 index companies, whom you believe have high growth prospects. In a marriage or partnership, one partner could take the ten-bagger route, while the other buys FTSE All-Share tracker units, again spreading the risks. If you plan to hold your shares for years, reinvesting your annual dividends will boost your holdings. Within an Isa plan, you will get a 10 per cent tax credit until it is phased out on 5 April 2004. One option would be to buy ten shares at an outlay of £500 each, for a total cost of £5,000 and balance this by opening a monthly savings plan for a FTSE All-Share tracker fund, increasing its value by regular payments over time. How the balanced portfolio shapes up is shown in the example below.

Creating a balanced portfolio

Year 1: April 2000–April 2001 – maxi self-select ISA

No. of shares	*Company*	*Initial cost*
133	Amvescap	£998
152	Next	£1,003
184	Celltech	£1,003
468	Smith & Nephew	£998
512	Tesco	£998
Total invested during the year		£5,000

Year 1: April 2000–April 2001 – FTSE All-Share tracker

£250 per month into M&G FTSE All-Share tracker

Total invested during the year	£3,000

Year 2: April 2001–April 2002 – maxi self-select ISA

No. of shares	*Company*	*Initial cost*
420	ARM Holdings	£1,008
200	Capita	£1,001
152	Man	£1,003

224	Phytopharm	£998
100	WPP	£990
Total invested during the year		£5,000

Year 2: April 2001–April 2002 – FTSE All-Share tracker
£300 per month into Prudential All-Share tracker

Total invested during the year	£3,600
Total investment from April 2000 to 2002	£16,600

The creation of a thousand forests is in one acorn
Ralph Waldo Emerson, American philosopher and poet

To achieve greater balance, add a few slower-growing companies who have regular, reliable earnings and pay consistent or rising dividends. This is a good foil for a high-growth ten-bagger portfolio. I use this approach, having eleven companies in my portfolio (one of which, Durlacher, is a leftover I hope might eventually recover). Only six are possible future ten-baggers: another five pay attractive and rising dividends to serve at a later date as extra income to supplement annual pensions. Owning high dividend-paying shares is like owning property that pays rent: they provide a reliable income every year. This grows more valuable over time and is exceptionally useful during periods of low interest rates or market downturns when capital growth is minimal. Slow-growing companies should, we hope, add capital growth if they are left quietly to continue growing over several years.

Another risk-reduction idea is to run two portfolios in parallel, buying shares in the four largest UK FTSE 100 index companies, to balance the ten-bagger portfolio. This immediately provides holdings in four of the UK's most successful sectors; BP in oils, GlaxoSmithKline in pharmaceuticals, Vodafone in mobile telecoms and HSBC in banks. Together, they account for about 25 per cent of the whole FTSE 100 index giving a broad spread by buying just four shares. BP, GlaxoSmithKline and HSBC have stable earnings and pay regular dividends on a rising trend. Vodafone is a growth company in one of the most exciting sectors, although it had debt problems and technical concerns over implementing new 3G (third generation) services during the 2001–2 economic slowdown. Vodafone as a possible ten-bagger is covered in Chapter 10.

Information overload

Having examined portfolio design, where should you search for ten-bagger candidates? When I began investing in 1990, the paucity of readily available information was matched only by my ignorance about how to access what information there was. I had little cash to spend on information, so I chose a minimum group; the daily *Financial Times*, the *Sunday Times* and *Investors Chronicle*, both published weekly, and *Money Observer*, published monthly. Later, I added two or three specialist newsletters but I no longer subscribe to any of these although my original collection of financial aids remains my core information sources, supplemented by a monthly hard copy of *Company Refs*, now available on the Internet, plus annual reports and websites. *Company Refs* is an invaluable compendium of fundamental information on every listed UK-based company, including all the AIM companies (quoted on the Alternative Investment Market). I prefer the hard copy version because I can look back several months to changes in the essential statistics of the companies I hold shares in or am following as future possible purchases.

Company annual and interim reports make useful reading and are free – a valuable guide when weighing up an investment. Even if the accounting details are over your head, statements by the chairman and chief executive are informative as are the headline facts on recent progress and events. Many UK companies have their own websites where news, share price information, company history and annual report details are posted.

I have stuck to my initial reading list because I am essentially conservative in my choice of reading. Yet this small collection shows investors do not need a huge amount of information. If success depended on information access, more institutional investors would produce excellent results. With relatively few aids it is possible to prepare and run a long-term wealth-creating portfolio, which is our priority objective.

A wealth of information creates a poverty of attention

Herbert Simon, economist

Essential reading kit for investors

1 One Daily Newspaper: the *Financial Times*, *The Times*, the *Telegraph*, the *Guardian*
2 One Sunday Newspaper: the *Sunday Times*, *Sunday Observer* or *Telegraph*
3 *Investors Chronicle*, published weekly
4 *Money Observer*, or *Bloomberg Money*, published monthly
5 *Company Refs*, published monthly; available on the Internet at www.hemscott.net

Today, we can suffer information overload, a complaint I have happily avoided by following the slogan, 'Keep it simple, stupid!' But for those who love the search, a plethora of informative websites, newsletters, TV programmes and radio coverage deal with everything financial. Useful books can be borrowed from the library, or bought for pennies at charity shops.

Other sources of financial information

Television programmes

1 CNBC: digital services

2. CNN: a wide range of financial programmes plus real-time news and business coverage on cable services
3. BBC: terrestrial television, breakfast and lunchtime programmes
4. Bloomberg: continuous financial and investment coverage on digital services
5. Sky: wide-ranging financial and investment coverage, on digital stations

News sources

1. Reuters: available on topic screens and websites
2. *Financial Times* websites:
   www.ftyourmoney.com
   www.FTMarketWatch.com
   www.FT.com, www.ft.com/cityline (FT Cityline for real time share prices)
3. *The Times*: websites
4. Market Eye (datastream) and Topic (Reuters) direct feeds from the London Stock Exchange, for real-time share prices, company and market information
5. Individual company websites, ideal for information and annual reports

Financial and investment websites

1. www.citywire.co.uk
2. Motley Fool at www.fool.com
3. CNN.com/business

Picking 'expert' brains

Among the largest brokerage houses, such as Goldman Sachs, Merrill Lynch and Morgan Stanley, a conflict arises between the need to provide impartial advice and boosting income fees from merger and acquisition activity. Fund managers are increasingly sceptical about relying on research by the investment banks as they may be biased towards buy recommendations. We saw in Chapter 3 how positive brokers were about Marconi even when other infrastructure equipment manufacturers reported immense difficulties. However, for ten-bagger treasure hunters buy recommendations are insightful, if they occur early. I used a buy note from the Companies & Markets section of the *Financial Times* to buy my first holding in Logica in December 1997 at 230p, long before it entered the FTSE 100 index, when it was recommended by a large brokerage firm whose name eludes me. I held Logica over the next year and realised it was an exciting long-term hold that might become a ten-bagger. Logica was profiled to illustrate FASTER GAINS in *The Wealthy Investor.* At the time of writing *Backing Winners*, it had issued three profit warnings and no longer looked attractive as a future ten-bagger company; but during the millennium bubble boom Logica reached 2,725p, more than fulfilling that early promise.

Life has nothing to do with luck.
The only place luck comes before work is in the dictionary
Anita Roddick, founder of Body Shop

Tracking broker recommendations

For the cost of a daily newspaper you may pick up useful snippets on broker insights about companies they are advising institutional investor clients to buy. Although fund managers say they pay less attention to such recommendations, market activity on the days influential brokers make them suggests otherwise: they often move prices.

Noting broker recommendations has three advantages. First, brokers do not know whether the markets are going to rise or fall. They might suggest buying on a day when companies issue profit warnings, or the general background is excessively pessimistic. You may be able to pick up your favoured shares more cheaply as prices fall across the market.

Second, many of their recommendations include target 'buy'

prices up to which price the broker thinks the shares are attractive, or longer-term target 'sell' prices towards which they might move. These prices give guidance on the profit possible if that 'sell' target is reached, perhaps three years ahead. I used the broker's 'buy' target as a first focus for my Logica holding in 1997. He thought Logica was good value up to 380p, an early price target to aim for. And third, if you buy before the institutions their buying can push prices up, helping your investment to show an early profit.

Brokers in overdrive

Tracking broker recommendations uncovers their preferences and offers helpful information on companies you may be following. So much information is freely available over the Internet, the financial press now details broker comments and recommendations within regular stock market reports. This is a great boon to investors who can obtain useful nuggets by routinely following these accounts.

On Friday 10 August 2001 the report on the London Stock Exchange on the back page of the Companies & Markets part of the *Financial Times* was a treasure store of recommendations. Here is a list of the companies, the brokers and their suggestions for that day:

Company	Broker	Recommendation
Balfour Beatty	Credit Lyonnais	Issued a pre-results 'buy' note at 151p
Balfour Beatty	Alastair Stewart	A premier league of UK construction cos. With Amec
Amec	Alastair Stewart	In the same premier league, with Balfour Beatty
Carillon	Alastair Stewart	Grouped with Balfour and Amec
Hanson	Credit Suisse First Boston	Downgrade to 'hold' from 'buy'

RMC	Credit Suisse First Boston	Downgrade to 'hold' with Hanson
GKN	Salomon Smith Barney	Trading at a sector discount at 297p, buy up to 360p
Pace Micro Tech	DKW	Pessimistic about short-term prospects
Vodafone	ING Barings	Downgrade from 'buy' to 'hold'
Colt Telecom	Bank of America	Cut price target from £25 to 700p, still a 'buy'
Guardian IT	Willams de Broe	Upgrade from 'hold' to 'buy'
Reed Intl	Deutsche Bank	Trading at 609p, 'buy' for a target price of 750–800p
Emap	Merrill Lynch	Downgrade to 'neutral' from 'accumulate'
Kingfisher	Teather & Greenwood	'Sell' on prospects for forthcoming demerger

A few days later, on 15 August, Balfour Beatty produced results that showed it was benefiting from increased government spending on infrastructure projects, in the UK and worldwide. The shares rose to 185p from the 150p they stood at before the broker recommendations, 23 per cent up in five days. This spectacular short-term rise illustrates the power that broker recommendations have to move markets.

Having scoured the sources of up-to-date information, the next big step is to compile a short-list of promising candidates, and how we search for them takes us on to Chapter 6.

Success is a lousy teacher

Bill Gates, chairman and 'chief software architect' of Microsoft

6 **Treasure Hunting**

I think it makes sense to have the small company bias if you are prepared to take a longer term view
Paul Whitney, head of Natwest Investment Management

With over 2,500 companies listed on the London Stock Exchange plus 800 more on AIM, and thousands of foreign firms, the choice looks overwhelming but it becomes more manageable by following a pre-set plan. The selection process also helps to tilt the odds towards success, through extensive filtering. In addition, using the ten-bagger profile soon whittles down the daunting totals. Indeed, the real problem is almost the reverse: among the huge choice in Britain alone, very few companies will become convincing winners and even less will achieve a resounding result. Ten-bagger companies are relatively so rare that the ten-bagger profile eliminates over 95 per cent of possible candidates, allowing you to focus your efforts on the remaining 5 per cent. Winnowing down the overall total produces a preliminary short-list of potential winners. After compiling a group of fifteen or twenty likely candidates, the next step is to select a portfolio of about ten, as I will explain in this chapter. I can offer only guidelines as, sadly, I have no crystal ball, although I am convinced new ten-baggers can still be found.

Aim for success

At the riskiest end of the spectrum is AIM (the Alternative Investment Market), which allows young companies to list on a public exchange for modest fees even though they have a shorter trading record than is required by the London Stock Exchange rules. It may seem contrary to begin by looking at this market, but for smart investors who have the time to pursue the details of AIM-listed firms, there are sure to be several with huge potential promise.

In the summer of 2001 AIM celebrated its sixth birthday. Since its launch in 1995 AIM has attracted over 800 companies from a range of sectors raising almost £7 billion. As a junior market for UK companies hoping to tap expansion funds, AIM has been a resounding success; its launch coincided with the great millennium boom. In 1999 it rose by an amazing 143 per cent: during 2000, 223 companies joined AIM's list, mainly exploiting the flourishing Internet bubble. AIM has less onerous admission policies than the main exchange with cheaper admission fees, helpful to cash-strapped young firms. Simon Brickles, chief operating officer, describes AIM as a no-nonsense market with relatively straightforward rules. Although it lists small, early-stage companies, the failure rate at 3 per cent is respectable.

The problem with common sense is that it is not very common

Anonymous

Company Refs covers the entire group by collecting monthly fundamental details on each one, a useful hunting ground. In addition to coverage by *Company Refs*, information about AIM companies features on numerous websites and in an *AIM Newsletter* produced by stockbroking firm Durlacher.

Feeling comfortable about following AIM-listed companies is an important aspect of your approach to risk. I personally no longer feel happy chasing small, untried companies, but this attitude has two causes: first, I do not want to dedicate the necessary time and investing without due diligence would be much riskier; second, I feel more comfortable with larger, more established companies. But for younger, energetic investors AIM could be a fruitful source of ten-bagger companies.

Searching for future FTSE 100 winners

For more cautious investors and for another source of possible ten-baggers, the lower places on the FTSE 100 list can throw up interesting companies, although their positions and rankings change with a surprisingly hectic frequency. For example, on 12 September 2001, when the investment community was reeling from the tragic terrorist attacks on America's financial and political heartlands, the FTSE committee announced one of the biggest quarterly shake-ups in the constituents of its three benchmark indices, the FTSE 100, 250 and SmallCap indices. Eight companies from the New Economy, spearheaded by Marconi were ejected from the FTSE 100 index, to be replaced by eight stalwart, traditional companies as shown below. There were eight promotions to the FTSE SmallCap index and nineteen exclusions, including several high technology companies. Among their number were several who had entered the FTSE 100 at the peak of the millennium boom in March 2000. The alternative telecoms supplier, Thus, was relegated, having fallen to rank 404, while many former favourites were languishing: Psion at 447, Bookham Technologies at 475 and Scipher at 530: other demotions included BATM Advanced Communications at 536 and Bioglan Pharma down at 548.

Some FTSE benchmark indices changes at close of business on 11 September 2001

New Entrants to FTSE 100	*Sector*	*Ranking*
Friends Provident	Life assurance	64
Enterprise Oil	Oil exploration	77
Wolseley	Building construction	82

	Sector	*Ranking*
Severn Trent	Water	87
British Land	Property	90
Man	Speciality and other finance	91
Northern Rock	Bank	92
Innogy	Electricity	94
Evictions from FTSE 100 to 250		
Carlton Communications	Media	114
Misys	Software and computer services	116
CMG	Support services	123
Colt Telecommunications	Telecommunication services	148
Telewest	Telecommunication services	152
Energis	Telecommunication services	160
Spirent	Information technology hardware	172

Down among the minnows

As the list of new entrants to the FTSE 100 index shows, the elevated companies were minnows, among the lowest twenty. Within the total 100 companies in the FTSE premier benchmark some well-established companies may be in decline; perhaps ICI, the specialist chemicals group (ranked 90) and Wolseley, a building supplier (newly elevated at 82). These cyclical companies experience difficulties during recessions when they struggle to make profits. But among those companies in the lowest twenty are some new entrants who could grow strongly over the next decade. It is here that future ten-baggers might be found.

The list I compiled in autumn 2001 to find a sample portfolio for *Backing Winners* is shown below. But it is for illustration purposes only, to outline the processes involved. Within six months, or less, the positions of these companies could probably look quite different as their rankings depend on market values, which are calculated daily by multiplying the share price by the number of shares in issue. Crucially, therefore, rankings depend on how popular or unpopular companies are with investors.

Failure is only the opportunity to begin again more intelligently

Henry Ford, founder of Ford Motor Car Company

Smaller FTSE 100 Companies (at 7 October 2001)

Company	*Ranking/ Is it rising or falling?*	*Business activity*	*Market cap (£ million)*	*Share price (p)*
ARM Holdings	78 Rising	IT equipment designer	2,767	273.5
Bradford & Bingley	95 Rising?	Banks	2,141	314
Capita Group	79 Rising	Outsourcing	2,708	411
Enterprise Oil	83 Static?	Oil exploration	2,532	518.5
ICI	93 Falling?	Chemicals	2,169	298
Man	87 Rising?	Fund manager	2,377	893
Next	70 Rising	General retailing	3,275	972
Ryanair*	98 Rising	Budget airline	2,021	576.5
Sage Group	96 Static?	Software provider	2,122	167.5
Schroders	94 Rising	Fund manager	2,159	733.5
Smith & Nephew	69 Rising	Health	3,419	373

Source: *Sunday Times*, Business Section

*Ryanair is based in Dublin and not eligible for FTSE 100 membership

Stage 1: Spotting promising candidates

Start by sifting through companies to find a group whose features seem to fit the ten-bagger profile, to compile a list of possible winners. When you have followed their fortunes over a period of six to nine months, the final selection of ten should emerge. To check how close the possible candidates are to the ten-bagger profile outlined in Chapter 2, you can look for certain clear features that might indicate their future potential.

Quick identity checks for possible ten-baggers

1. Have you heard of the chief executive? If so, he should be an important element of the company's success profile
2. Does the company operate in a fast-growing market sector?
3. Is it a niche market which may deter competitors?
4. Is it well known as the leading company in its sector?
5. Does it produce cash generative products?
6. Has it got small debts?
7. Is there a recognisable brand?
8. Does it have plenty of important clients? This information appears in the company's annual report, as firms are proud of their major client bases
9. Does the company rely heavily on a key product, market or customer?
10. Has it got a reputation for developing new products?

Open a file for each of the possible candidates you decide to follow, including companies whose shares you may already hold. Remain alert for news items, interim or final results announcements or coverage by brokers, as we noted in Chapter 5. Over the course of several months you will learn a great deal about these companies and begin to acquire a preference for some at the expense of others. This is exactly the process that I adopted to find a preliminary short-list and then winnow it down to a final selection that contained only ten.

In addition to companies I held in my personal portfolio, here is the group of prospects I collected during the summer of 2001. Again, this list is only a guide to show the process of choosing future ten-bagger companies.

Guardian IT I had followed Guardian IT's flotation in early 1999, but as there were numerous flotations in the high technology and support services sectors, I could not decide which were worth pursuing. A note in the Companies & Markets section of the *Financial Times* on 14 September 2001 drew my attention back to Guardian IT and it went on to my list for its potential ten-bagger status.

Man Group I discovered this interesting company early in 2001. It is an international hedge fund manager and futures broker. Hedge funds became hugely popular during the 1990s boom, hot favourites for high-worth private investors in America and Britain, hoping for annual returns above 15 to 20 per cent. This figure seems high but is possible for aggressively run funds. When hedge funds emerged in the 1960s, they adopted a conservative approach to risk, buying shares they thought would rise and offsetting them by selling shares they considered over-valued. This balanced or 'hedged' approach gave them their name and proved extremely profitable. During the 1970s some hedge funds adopted higher risk strategies, taking big bets in one direction only. This ploy became world renowned when George Soros, among the world's most celebrated speculators, nearly broke the Bank of England in 1992; by selling sterling against the Bank he made $1 billion.

This is the sector where Man is creating an increasingly global presence. When it was elevated to the FTSE 100 index in September 2001, it had £5.8 billion funds under management, up from £5.4 billion since the previous June, with funds rising at the rate of 13.6 per cent over three months. Having raised its funds 60 per cent to £4.7 billion during its last financial year, to 31 March 2001, Man planned to double its managed funds in three years. With strong demand from private clients and institutions, assets under management reached £6.6 billion by 31 October. The shares had almost doubled since 2 January 2001 rising from 616p to 1,215p by 8 November. Man became another prospect on my preliminary short-list.

It takes years to make an overnight success

Eddie Cantor, American singer of the 1930s

Smith & Nephew was an unfocused poorly managed healthcare group in the mid-1990s before it embarked upon a three-year vigorous restructuring, to reinvent itself as a high-technology medical devices company. This refocused the group on proven growth sectors, and it promised to deliver mid-teens earnings growth in 2002 and beyond. In an optimistic trading statement in mid-June 2001 Smith & Nephew reported its progress. Like-for-like growth across the group was 12 per cent in the first half, but 18 per cent when adding in recent acquisitions. Its best area was orthopaedics – artificial hips and knees, where sales growth of 15 per cent compared with 9 per cent in 2000. Growth here will be underpinned by the demographic profile of an active but ageing population and the government's commitment to improve health provision, injecting about £3 billion of new money into the National Health Service. However, against this potential is the possibility that overstretched UK hospitals will be unable to provide the operations. If patients go to France or Germany for hip replacements and other surgery, Smith & Nephew will not gain the benefit of rising sales for its orthopaedic products. Anticipating a revival in Smith & Nephew's growth the share price rose during 2000, taking its ranking up through the FTSE 250 list and entry into the FTSE 100 index.

Oasis Healthcare was featured at 39.5p in the *Sunday Times* on 9 September 2001. This small AIM-listed company provides dental services, a virtually recession-proof area: people with toothache seek professional relief from pain. During 2001 the government announced plans to put more cash into the sector. Since flotation in 2000, Oasis had assembled nearly fifty practices and was expected to report a maiden profit in 2001. Margins could improve with expansion. Oasis has defensive qualities plus growth potential, making it a suitable candidate to follow. I cannot imagine dental patients going abroad for treatment, but you never know!

Celltech was the UK's first FTSE 100 biotechnology group, recently joined by Shire Pharmaceuticals. Celltech's expertise is in producing genetically engineered antibodies and other leading-edge drugs. Its quality intellectual property portfolio is reflected in rapidly growing royalty income from other companies. In 2001 it had a pipeline of twelve products and the antibody treatment for rheumatoid arthritis, partnered by US titan Pharmacia, had excellent potential, based on trials, coupled with low production costs.

Following Celltech's acquisition of Medeva, the sales force for its once-a-day treatment of Metadate CD for hyperactive children was increased to expand the US market share from 4 per cent. Revenues from Metadate CD sales should provide around $150 million annually at its peak, but Celltech's greater resources rely on new products in its pipeline plus ambitions for a pan-European expansion. This was signalled by its acquisition of Thiemann, a German pharmaceuticals marketing company to boost the European sales force and strengthen its European network. These moves make it more attractive as the partner of choice for US biotechnology companies wanting to break into the European market. When Celltech produced strong interim figures in September 2001 Deutsche Bank stuck to its price target of 1,120p, a rise of 36 per cent from the 823p at which it was trading.

Synergy Healthcare was acquired from receivers in 1991 by the management that had restored it to profitability. It provides specialised outsourced medical support services for the National Health Service through long-term contracts. Synergy had negotiated thirty-four contracts with NHS trusts, which provide secure income over several years. It had a record £40 million current order book and was tendering for a further eighteen contracts worth a total of £6 million. The market for Synergy's services is huge and due to expand in response to government plans to increase spending on health services. The trend from in-house to outsourced services is expanding rapidly across the economy, from plastic and paper packaging for the supermarket chains, to the financial services that Capita Group supplies. Synergy should therefore benefit from this growing trend. It joined AIM early in August 2001, at 128p per share. The offer was oversubscribed, attracting support from some of the UK's major fund management groups, and raised £8 million to fund future expansion.

As with other AIM-listed companies, the shares can be difficult to trade; with only 16 million in issue, most are in the firm hands of founders and institutions. House broker Brewin Dolphin expected Synergy to report sales of £12.5 million and profits of £1.5 million for 2002, rising to £17 million and £2.25 million respectively for 2003. With the price at 191p the shares had risen 63p, nearly 50 per cent within one month, putting them on a forward p/e (price/earnings ratio) of 21, a fairly high rating. Synergy is an ideal candidate to watch for a few weeks to see how the share price settles after the initial flotation excitement.

Phytopharm According to Erling Refsum of Nomura, nearly half the medicines discovered during the twentieth century came from herbal remedies. He thought Phytopharm, a specialist developing new medical treatments from herbal compounds, had a promising future as it is re-inventing already-known remedies. One medicine, an appetite suppressor, was being developed in conjunction with US drugs giant Pfizer.

Galen is an interesting FTSE 250 company: a small, fast-growing drugs group based in Northern Ireland. I first found Galen when scanning for interesting ten-bagger companies in *Company Refs.* We will consider it further in Chapter 7.

Nobody wants to pay a big entry fee for a game with a small prize
Michael Mandel, author of *The Coming Internet Depression*

Restructured giants

As mentioned earlier, young or small companies can be much riskier investments than larger more established firms, although this is by no means invariably true. However, when choosing a ten-bagger portfolio, it is clearly preferable to adopt the least risky options. Hence, looking first at larger companies remains the most cautious route. Some giant companies in the past have proved adept at re-inventing themselves to improve their profitability. IBM is one such titan with a surprising ability to adapt rapidly to changing conditions. By re-engineering its basic business model it had made repeated comebacks despite intense competition. Other contenders might include BP, having adopted a 'clean fuels' policy; Tesco, the supermarket group with the most successful and profitable Internet grocery shopping business; WPP, the global advertising giant crippled by debts in the early 1990s. Amvescap, a FTSE 100 fund management group, is in this category, as it stands high up in the FTSE 100 index, and is growing aggressively through its acquisitions.

Or consider Woolworths. On 28 August 2001 Kingfisher, the high street retailer, demerged its Woolworths subsidiary as a separate company. As part of the demerger, the newly floated business was saddled with high debts due to e-commerce losses, high rental costs and a massive stock overhang of £100 million. It had yet to appoint a new chief executive to run daily operations. The new executive chairman, Gerald Corbett, was confident that once the e-commerce losses were staunched the company's fortunes could be substantially revived by introducing strong budgeting disciplines. He hoped to expand the core store operations with as many as 150 new locations, arguing that while out-of-town supermarkets were popular, there was a place for high street stores catering for low-cost basic items, especially at Christmas. To promote the company and get the demerger off to a successful start he toured institutional fund managers.

In 2000, a bad year for high street general merchandise retailers, Woolworths reported profits of £95 million on sales of £2.5 billion, indicating plenty of activity by shoppers along Britain's high streets, although profits were low. At 25p, as forecast by the 'grey market' ahead of the demerger, the prospective dividend yield would be an appetising 6 per cent, but the estimated value was a lowly £350 million, well below earlier valuation hopes, while Gerald Corbett had warned that Woolworths needed a major overhaul.

The low share price for the demerged group reflected investors' worries over fierce competition in its key sectors; entertainment and confectionery, putting its market leadership under pressure. Woolworths two strongest rivals were Tesco and Wal-Mart. Investors worried about the huge inventory overhang; stock clearance would hit profits short-term but could cut working capital by £100 million. Losses in e-commerce would need to be stemmed at its speciality 'Big W' stores and an attractive range of goods brought quickly on to the shelves for the Christmas trade. An important early clue to fast progress would be how quickly the £300 million debt could be wiped out with the end of January 2002 as a feasible target. Another would be whether profit margins could be lifted to around 5 per cent.

When a company becomes unpopular and its share price tumbles, the arrival of an energetic new boss and management team could signal recovery. This is precisely the kind of situation where ten-baggers can arise because the conditions for a revival are in place but investors are too negative to support the company. Like the bargains Woolworths is famous for providing on the high street, if shares could be bought cheaply, they might prove to be an investment bargain for patient investors. People living in towns across Britain would all be able to judge the progress of the newly independent Woolworths by popping into their local store to check on the goods on offer and how many people were queuing to pay at the checkouts. The opening low for the share price was 25p and it ended the first day of trading at 31.5p.

As history has shown, success includes its weak spots

Møerk Hallstein, senior vice-president, Human Resources, Nokia

Backing survivors

Brokers are professional experts who spend their lives researching companies for their institutional clients. This gives them a powerful insight into how companies are performing and what their future potential might be. Since information became more freely available on the Internet, the financial press has begun to feature their observations and recommendations on a more regular basis. Staying alert to companies that brokers recommend is useful when searching for future winners. The year 2000 saw an explosion of interest in small, start-up companies, especially in technology sectors. Jeremy Batstone, head of research at NatWest Stockbrokers, was cautious; numerous companies meant fierce competition and many would fail. Yet there will be survivors, and among these canny investors should search for future ten-baggers.

Merrill Lynch tipped three technology survivors as big winners: Vodafone, Logica, the software company, and ARM Holdings, the chip designer. Coincidentally, all three were then in my portfolio. HSBC also tipped Vodafone and Logica, with Spirent, a telecoms equipment tester, and Sage Group, the accounting software company, on its winners' list. Here, as earlier noted, I held Sage but not Spirent, which was relegated from the FTSE 100 index in September 2001. Both strategists were optimistic that their technology favourites would soar when the global economy recovered from the severe 2001 slump.

Stage II: Sifting through the short-list

My short-list of eighteen possible choices, shown below, was compiled during the summer of 2001. The pace of change in the spheres of commerce and business is now so rapid that it is not possible to say how relevant this list will remain. It is given for guidance only on how ten-bagger hunters should proceed. The next stage is to sift through the companies on the preliminary short-list to whittle the choice down to ten candidates. The most constructive way to do this is to perform a ten-bagger profile assessment on each company in turn, before making the final selection.

My preliminary short-list

Company	*Sector*
(i) Amvescap	Speciality and other finance
(ii) ARM Holdings	Information technology hardware
(iii) Capita Group	Support services
(iv) Celltech Group	Pharmaceuticals
(v) Galen	Pharmaceuticals
(vi) Guardian IT	Software and computer services
(vii) IG Group	Speciality and other finance
(viii) Logica	Software and computer services
(ix) Man	Speciality and other finance
(x) Next	General retailers
(xi) Oasis Healthcare	AIM (healthcare)
(xii) Phytopharm	Pharmaceuticals

(xiii) Ryanair Hldgs	Transport
(xiv) Sage Group	Software and computer services
(xv) Smith & Nephew	Healthcare
(xvi) Synergy Healthcare	AIM (healthcare)
(xvii) Vodafone	Telecommunication services
(xviii) Woolworths	General retailers

The final decision on which companies to support and which to eliminate from the short-list will depend on personal preferences. You may feel positive about healthcare companies or the high-technology sector. Having bought your chosen ten, by continuing to track the others on the preliminary short-list, you may decide to add another one or two later, if the story continues to look promising or as a replacement if you have to sell one of your early choices because it has failed to live up to initial expectations, a point we will cover in more detail in Chapter 9, Keep Tracking.

The breakdown in my preliminary short-list includes the following sectors, making a total of ten different sectors among eighteen companies.

Sector selections in the short-list

Sector	*Number of shares*
AIM	2
Information technology hardware	1
General retailers	2
Healthcare	1
Pharmaceuticals	3
Speciality and other finance	2
Support services	1
Software and computer services	3
Telecommunication services	1
Transport	1
Total number of sectors	10

No great achievement happens by luck alone
David Teng, Hong Kong businessman

As noted in Chapter 5, a broad spread of sectors helps to reduce risk. A minimum of seven sectors should feature in a portfolio of ten shares to maintain a diversified spread. This requirement alone helps when reducing the short-list down to a manageable group of ten. If, like me, you hold other shares in a more balanced portfolio, the sectors covered there will be an added factor to consider, especially if your existing portfolio already holds companies in one sector, for example general retailing, or transport.

Below, in brief, are the reasons why I decided to eliminate the companies that did not feature in my sample ten-bagger portfolio. These reasons take account of my existing portfolio, to ensure a broad spread plus my personal attitude to risk. The elimination list offers an idea of how investors should approach sifting out some of their first selections, after assessing each ten-bagger profile, to arrive at a final ten portfolio candidates. In choosing not to follow some companies, there is, of course, no guarantee that they will not go on to become excellent future ten-baggers.

In December 2001 Guardian IT produced their second profit warning of the year and although it had been put on my final candidate list, I immediately removed it and substituted Man Group, the specialist fund management group. As I had been following the Ten-point Action Plan for only six months, the possibility is strong that I would have still been in the 'watch-the-progress' stage of making my ten final choices. By substituting Man Group for Guardian IT we can see how valuable is the suggestion of following your chosen candidates for at least ten months to one year before you buy any companies – to be sure you have plenty of information about their past progress and possible future performance.

Your initial portfolio need not be rigid; if the growth story of one candidate began to flag, Man might then be a suitable replacement, as long as it was still growing and could be bought at a reasonable price.

Reason for removal of eliminated selections

(iv) Celltech Group	I held shares in Medeva in 1995 and did not want to own it again as would have been the case, since Celltech had acquired Medeva
(vi) Guardian IT	I was unwilling to buy shares in a company that had produced two profit warnings in 2001, but Guardian IT stayed on my substitute 'watch' list
(viii) Logica	Issued three profit warnings in autumn 2001 and spring 2002. Relegated from FTSE 100 index in June 2002.
(xi) Oasis Healthcare	I thought an AIM healthcare company would be risky
(xii) Phytopharm	I was not sufficiently impressed by the story
(xv) Smith & Nephew	I decided it might not grow strongly enough to become a ten-bagger
(xvi) Synergy Healthcare	For me, an AIM pharmaceuticals company was too risky
(xvii) Vodafone	Covered separately as a possible ten-bagger in Chapter 10
(xviii) Woolworths	I did not rate the recovery potentials highly enough to generate a ten-bagger return

In the next chapter we take a detailed look at the profiles of the ten-baggers that I selected.

People forget today's junk is tomorrow's blue chip

Michael Milken, inventor of junk bonds

7 The Ten-bagger Portfolio

Great stocks are extremely hard to find. If they weren't then everyone would own them. I knew I wanted to own the best or none at all

Philip Fisher, American investment guru

In Chapter 6 I reduced my preliminary short-list of eighteen prospects down to ten, listed below. My sample ten-bagger portfolio includes six shares I own; several will not be ten-baggers for me as I bought them at too high a starting price. The list looked promising in late 2001, but includes risky small companies. Growth stories might collapse or share prices surge by the time *Backing Winners* is published. My selection may not be relevant or suitable to every investor; it is for guidance only. The fundamental data given for each company refer to 29 October 2001. As space is limited, only four of the ten are covered with a complete ten-bagger winner's profile.

With pension and retirement issues a growing consideration for me personally, I naturally have adopted a more cautious attitude towards the total composition of my existing portfolio. Although I follow the fortunes of the four companies I do not personally hold shares in – Galen, Man Group, Next and Ryanair – I do not want to increase the total number of companies in my portfolio beyond around twelve. The six companies in which I do hold shares are marked † in the table below.

Company	*Sector*	*Price 29.12.00*	*Price 29.10.01*
(i) Amvescap†	Speciality and other finance	1,374p	887p
(ii) ARM Holdings†	Information technology hardware	506p	345p
(iii) Capita Group (The)†	Support services	500p	460p
(iv) Galen	Pharmaceuticals	843p	745p
(v) IG Group†	Speciality and other finance	548p	578p
(vi) Man Group	Speciality and other finance	616p	1,135p
(vii) Next	General retailer	805p	860p
(viii) Ryanair	Transport	715p	636p*
(ix) Sage Group†	Software and computer services	307p	213p
(x) Vodafone†¶	Telecommunications	246p	163p

*In December 2001 Ryanair had a 'share split'. Subsequently, each share was divided into two. The revised price by December was therefore 318p, as shown on page 133, where the fundamental features of Ryanair are given as part of its ten-bagger profile.

†Companies where I have a shareholding.

¶Covered in Chapter 10.

Ten Ten-bagger portfolio candidates

Amvescap

Sector: Speciality and other finance
Market cap: £6,990 million
Share price: 887p
Ranking: 38
Index: FTSE 100
52-week high/low: 1,590p–596p

Forecast earnings:	P/E
2002: 43.8p	20.3
2003: 50p (assuming 15 per cent increase)	17.7

Amvescap became one of the UK's largest fund management groups when it was formed in 1997 by the merger of London-based Invesco and Houston-based AIM (no connection with the Alternative Investment Market). In 2001 Amvescap was the fifth largest US collective funds provider and made 91 per cent of its profits in America. It had grown through a vigorous acquisitions policy, and had a wide range of products, with Invesco and AIM as its flagship trusts.

In summer 2001, although the economic downturn seemed widespread, Amvescap was optimistic about recovery, despite steep declines in equity markets and a massive drain from US mutual funds. Estimates for profits in 2002 were forecast to be in the region of £500 million.

I was first attracted by Amvescap's March 2001 full year results and press comments on its prospects. It had fallen from a high of around 1,735p in November 2000. I paid over 1,000p for my holding but expect the shares to double in value over the next few years. However, they might produce a ten-bagger result for investors who buy at lower prices. I knew the shares would be volatile during 2001 because it is operationally geared to the performance of the US and UK stock markets. The value of funds under management fluctuates wildly while the cost base remains fairly rigid. As the US equity markets recover, so will Amvescap's share price.

As one of only a few independent fund management groups Amvescap has a scarcity value and could become a takeover target, adding to its attractions for investors.

Ten-bagger profile of Amvescap

Visionary chief executive with a sound business plan Charles W.

Brady, chief executive of Amvescap, founded the US-based group in 1978 and then grew it into a leading global fund management group worth over £5,400 million. His visionary business plan was based on a laser-like money management focus. In the words of Robert McCullough, Amvescap's chief financial officer, 'We're able to take all of our cash flow and use it to get the best people, the best technology and the best customer service.'

Operates in a market with huge future growth potential Unlike many competitors, Amvescap focuses exclusively on investment management, its core business. The fund management industry has expanded over recent years as more people seek professional management for savings and investments. Future growth looks doubly secure as increasing numbers save for long-term financial needs, especially lengthy retirements. In *The Roaring 2000s*,* Harry S. Dent argued convincingly about a high US spending boom that he thought was set to peak in 2010, when American 'baby boomers' (part of a population boom that occurred during the twenty years following the end of the Second World War in 1945), now aged forty to forty-nine reduce their spending and focus on retirement saving. Amvescap should be well placed to benefit from that long-term shift. Growth will come from its global spread and further expansion of the long-term savings market. Amvescap is quoted on five stock markets: London, New York, Paris, Frankfurt and Tokyo.

Niche market with high entry costs to deter competitors A limited number of major fund management groups operate in the fund management sector; their prosperity often depends on the performance of a few gifted managers. This limits entry to the market by rivals. As of 30 June 2001 Amvescap had £289.6 billion ($408.4 billion) in client funds and was one of the world's largest

* Harry S. Dent, *The Roaring 2000s*, Simon & Schuster, 1998.

investment management firms. Over the past five years, it had achieved an excellent average 90 per cent return on equity.

Opportunity to be the leading company in its sector By 2001 Amvescap was the fifth largest mutual funds manager in the US and Canada, having acquired Canadian group Trimark early in 2000. Headquartered in Atlanta, Georgia, it had forty offices in twenty-five countries with clients in more than 100 countries – a global business. It had ambitions to become the leading fund manager in its markets. Executive chairman, Charles W. Brady, says: 'We think this strategy of local service with global resources is exactly right for the future and distinguishes us from the crowd.'

Highly cash generative products and cash in the bank Fund management is highly cash generative as fees are taken from funds under management before distribution to investors or shareholders. Funds however can fluctuate greatly in volatile markets. In 2001 Amvescap had net cash of 56.1p per share.

Low debt levels Amvescap had relatively low levels of debt.

Potential to build a powerful brand Amvescap had been operating in its current form only since 1997, but as a major fund management group in America and Britain, it had the potential to build a powerful brand.

Large and expanding pool of contracts, clients, markets Analysts were impressed by the resilience Amvescap showed in its core brands, AIM and Invesco, and its recent acquisitions, made to plug holes in its product range, including the purchase of Trimark and Perpetual. Its presence in fixed income products (bonds) has expanded. These proved popular as investors fled equity funds during 2001. By autumn estimates suggested 75 per cent of new money went into money market rather than equity products. If Amvescap can increase the volumes of funds in its fixed income products, the revenue stream will become less volatile. Future growth for Amvescap could come from more bolt-on acquisitions of smaller rivals. In 2001 further acquisitions included Pell Rudman, a US high net-worth specialist, Taiwanese fund manager Grand Pacific and UK property adviser Parkes & Co. Each acquisition adds funds under management: these three added $10.2 billion during the third quarter.

Not dependent solely on one key product, market or client Amvescap had developed a diverse product range in addition to its two core strong brands, Invesco and AIM.

Ability to evolve and develop new innovative products Amvescap could continue to introduce new types of funds, including hedge funds, money market or property funds.

ARM Holdings

Sector: Information technology hardware
Market cap: £3,491 million
Share price: 345p
Ranking: 65
Index: FTSE 100
52-week high/low: 567p–201p

Forecast earnings:	P/E
2002: 4.35p	79.3
2003: 5.2p (assumes 20 per cent increase)	66.3

I first started following ARM Holdings in the summer of 2000, when the share price was fluctuating around 800p. At that level, ARM had a price/earnings ratio of 236.6 on forecast earnings of 3.38p for 2001 and a p/e of 184 for forecast earnings of 4.35p for

2002. This was clearly an excessive overvaluation; it kept me firmly on the sidelines watching the price action, while hoping a future opportunity would emerge so I could buy shares in this innovative and fast-growing group. I personally think that of all the companies featured in *Backing Winners*, ARM Holdings had the most encouraging ten-bagger profile in 2001, mainly because it was still growing strongly, despite the economic downturn, but the price had fallen back steeply along with those of all the other companies listed in the technology sectors.

By 2001 ARM Holdings was at the forefront of pioneering technology, the leading provider of the 16/32-bit embedded RISC chips; these core microprocessor solutions were increasingly finding a place in an ever-increasing number of applications. The processors are high-performance, low-cost and power-efficient and are licensed to users so ARM has no manufacturing facility, just an ongoing stream of licence fees and royalty payments. Increasingly, they were replacing slower, 8-bit microprocessors across whole sectors of manufactured products.

ARM was a great UK technology success story. It had been a quoted company only since 17 April 1998 when it demerged from parent Acorn Computers, to float on the London Stock Exchange with a market value around £275 million. An investment of £1,000 on flotation would have been worth £19,240 at a price of 370p by mid-November 2001, an impressive growth exceeding 1,824 per cent in three and a half years.

Despite the exponential growth rate, there could be more progress because in October 2001, when the whole US technology sector was suffering from downgrades and reduced revenues, ARM Holdings announced impressive third quarter results. As it was then still a young relatively undeveloped company with a modest market capitalisation, operating in a fast-growing sector of the information technology industry, the future looked very positive.

In June 2002, however, shares in the chip sector plunged when

Intel, the market leader, revised down expected revenues, suggesting recovery for the sector would be futher delayed.

A dream can steer you through a lifetime of realities
Richard Wilkins, *The Yellow Book*

Ten-Bagger profile of ARM Holdings

Visionary chief executive with a sound business plan Visionary executive chairman Robin Saxby was at the forefront of ARM's early success having developed a strong business plan based on licences and royalty payments as repeatable revenues for ARM's pioneering designs. He had a large personal stake in the company, giving him additional motivation for its future success. During its early development phase, ARM paid no dividends, preferring to plough back all revenues to further develop the business. Saxby maintains: 'We have to continue to be smart and to innovate; if we fail to do that we become a dinosaur and die.'

Operates in a market with huge future growth potential ARM operates in the miniature microprocessor market, which in the early 2000s had huge future growth possibilities.

Niche market with high entry costs to deter competitors ARM operates in the niche market for low-cost, high-performance microchips, its core product. High entry costs deter competitors. Awkward lock-in to new technologies and high costs of switching enforce its niche market position.

Opportunity to be the leading company in its sector ARM was a world leader in its field but does face larger US rivals. It claimed to be market leader in the embedded microprocessor field.

Highly cash generative products and cash in the bank With no manufacturing facility, ARM relies on licences and revenues per chip sold, which were highly cash generative, to provide substantial cash flows. By September 2001 cash balances had risen to £102.2 million from £94.8 million at the end of the second quarter.

Low debt levels ARM had very low levels of debts.

Potential to build a powerful brand The company is well positioned to build a global brand; ARM's products could become global market standards.

Large and expanding pool of contracts, clients, markets ARM has a large and expanding pool of licensees and is continually adding new contracts and clients, including many US giants of the IT (information technology) industry.

Not dependent solely on one key product, market or client ARM is not dependent solely on one key product, market or client: its great strength derives from a wide diversity of products dependent on its own core microprocessor designs. As we saw with the ten-bagger profile of Nokia, this is an excellent format for strong growth as it relies on a versatile core product that can be widely applied to generate the diversity to avoid the problem of overdependence on one key product.

Ability to evolve and develop new innovative products The ability to evolve new products is crucial to the issue of avoiding overdependence on one core product. ARM has a large research and development budget; around one quarter of revenues are ploughed back into researching new designs. It collaborates with academic researchers at six universities, including Cambridge, where ARM is based, and Liverpool, where Robin Saxby had been an undergraduate. As he observed: 'Each university has got something slightly different to offer.' ARM has the ability to develop new innovative products and expand its client base worldwide. A medium-term ambition was to enter the health monitoring and biotechnology fields. This would be a major new departure with exciting long-term possibilities for additional growth.

Capita Group

Sector: Support services
Market cap: £3,402 million
Ranking: 74
Index: FTSE 100
Share price: 460p
52-week high/low: 527p–363p

Forecast earnings:	P/E
2002: 9.14p	50.3
2003: 10.5p (assumes 15 per cent increase)	43.8

Capita is an impressive group. I first began watching it in the late 1990s but as I was holding shares in Xansa, a smaller rival, I was not keen to hold Capita as well. However, Xansa had difficulties integrating a large acquisition during 2000 which knocked its profits. When I finally sold my holding, I decided to buy shares in Capita Group, the UK sector leader.

Rod Aldridge, executive chairman of Capita was truly a self-made man. Without a university education he began work at sixteen and trained in his spare time as a chartered public accountant. Qualified by the age of twenty-three, he worked through a series of white-collar positions. At the age of forty, in 1987 he struck out on his own, and organised the £300,000 buyout of a small consultancy, CCS, which offered advice to councils on routine issues such as computerising their payrolls. The move was a huge gamble, involving a second mortgage on his home, but self-belief is a powerful driver, as he observed: 'There was no way I was going to fail.' From this modest beginning Capita grew to become Britain's leading independent provider of outsourced back-office services for the public and private sectors, with a company payroll of 12,500 employees.

Outsourcing is a wide and varied area but Capita has focused on the fast-growing business market, which has huge future potential. Capita provides routine administrative chores for both private and public companies who want to avoid employing expensive technology teams to run their own day-to-day administration. Companies can make large savings when Capita runs these mundane tasks, so they increasingly turn to outsourcers.

The strength of Capita's outsourcing niche is a great asset with recurring long-term contracts announced with amazing regularity. New contracts worth £700 million were won in 2000; one was for £400 million to set up and run the Criminal Records Bureau for the Home Office over ten years. In January 2001 Capita won a breakthrough contract to provide back-office services for the Abbey National bank, worth £323 million over the next ten years. Rod Aldridge had targeted financial services as a new area for Capita to expand into, as financial outsourcing could be worth £8 billion. New contracts in the first five months of 2001 exceeded £720 million. Revenue growth for 2001 was forecast at 49 per cent, including underlying organic growth of 27 per cent after deducting for last year's acquisitions. In late October Capita announced new contracts worth up to £130 million and said prospects for the rest of the year remained 'excellent' with revenue growth likely to rise by 52 per cent.

One disturbing incident came to light in January 2002, when the government was forced to close its ambitious training scheme – Individual Learning Accounts – run by Capita, as fraudsters were exploiting lax controls. To maintain confidence in its efficiency, Capita would have to show the fault was due to a breach of trust among training providers, rather than a breach of Capita's security. The government is one of its most lucrative clients and flaws in its systems could jeopardise future contracts.

In 2001 Capita reported annual earnings had grown by more than 34.8 per cent since 1996. If this spectacular record of 90 per cent renewal on all its contracts continued, the share price could reach 1,000p by about 2005. But to become a ten-bagger, the share price must rise to 4,980p by 2011, which would involve a prodigious growth rate.

Although that target looks impossible, most small companies grow big through taking over rivals: they stay big and successful by integrating those acquisitions seamlessly into their main operations. Capita had a sensible acquisitions policy that had added to its core growth over several years. Its executive chairman, Rod Aldridge, says confidently: 'We are doubling in size every two-and-a-half years and expect to continue to do so.'

Vision without action is a daydream.
Action without vision is a nightmare
Japanese proverb

Ten-Bagger profile of Capita Group

Visionary chief executive with a sound business plan Visionary chief executive Rod Aldridge had a strong business franchise and more than a decade-long proven track record of growth.

Operates in a market with huge future growth potential Capita operates in the high technology business-process outsourcing market, which had massive growth potential, estimated in 2001 by Rod Aldridge at £50 billion: £30 billion of public sector opportunities and £20 billion from the private sector.

Niche market with high entry costs to deter competitors Outsourcing has become a high-skill industry. It is based on a company's ability to streamline repetitive processes and achieve overhead reductions to pass through to clients. An estimated £50 million a year in costs can be saved by organisations that sub-contract services to Capita.

Opportunity to be the leading company in its sector Capita was already the UK's leading independent outsourcing provider.

Highly cash generative products and cash in the bank Continuation of contracts that span several years gave Capita balance sheet strength and ability to generate repetitive earnings.

Low debt levels Many companies with high cash generation from routine operations had intentionally acquired moderate debt levels during the 1990s as a deliberate policy for improving their financial strength. Modest gearing (or borrowing) is beneficial to the performance of a company's assets. Capita adopted this policy and set out its reasons in the 2000 Annual General Report.

Potential to build a powerful brand Although the company was a back-office provider of services, an estimated 30 million British people were touched by the operations that Capita performed in 2000. The company was still comparatively small and its brand could become more important if growth continues.

Large and expanding pool of contracts, clients, markets Increasing numbers of organisations are outsourcing their routine back-office functions. As the business-process market is so huge, Capita had no plans to expand overseas or into such other areas as frontline services in health and education, but the potential exists there.

Not dependent solely on one key product, market or client In the first half of the financial year ending 2002, Capita announced it had won contracts worth £722 million, exceeding the total value of contracts in the previous year. Capita was targeting a new sector, the financial services industry, where there is a vast potential to sign up new clients and new contracts. In December 2001 Capita won its biggest-ever contract, for £500 million over ten years in a public sector deal to handle licence services for the BBC, a contract previously fulfilled by the Post Office.

Ability to evolve and develop new innovative products: Outsourcing is an expanding industry and the potential for developing new products not only already exists, it could increase over time.

It is better to be a has-been than a never-was

Lord Parkinson, British politician

Galen

Sector: Pharmaceuticals
Market cap: £1,382 million
Share price: 745p
Ranking: 130
Index: FTSE 250
52-week high/low: 962p–525p

Forecast earnings:	P/E
2002: 29.2p	25.5
2003: 33.6p	22.2

Galen was a popular favourite with analysts and brokers during 2000–2001 and caught my attention, although I do not personally own shares in the group. We introduced Galen, a small, fast-growing FTSE 250 Irish pharmaceuticals group, in Chapter 6. Since floating in 1997 it had expanded through a series of acquisitions. Turnover had more than doubled, from £39.3 million in 1997 to £86 million in 2000; pre-tax profits grew from £11 million to

£24.4 million and earnings per share rose from 6.13p in 1996 to 16.1p in 2000. Could this impressive growth continue with Galen integrating new acquisitions without major problems? We saw in Chapter 3 how rapid or unsuitable acquisitions can act like a lethal Exocet for the future growth of companies, large or small. Just look at the fate that befell Marconi and Baltimore Technologies.

In July 2001 three directors at Galen sold around £90 million in shares to increase liquidity in the free float of available shares, dropping their combined holdings from 42 per cent to 28 per cent, but this still left them with a large proportion of the equity. Investors should take careful note of how large director holdings are, as a balanced percentage is better than too large or too small a proportion. The directors sold shares to fund the acquisition of Estrace tablets, a hormone replacement therapy from Bristol-Myers Squibb. Galen announced a £200 million open offer of new shares to pay £67.2 million to fund this and future purchases. Analysts were optimistic about Galen's future prospects.

We are what we repeatedly do.
Excellence, then, is not an act, but a habit
Aristotle, Greek philosopher

IG Group

Sector: Speciality and other finance
Market cap: £312 million
Share price: 578p
Ranking: 316
Index: FTSE SmallCap
52-week high/low: 573p–464p

Forecast earnings:	P/E
2002: 24.1p	24
2003: 31.3p	18.5

Bet against the punters

At a time when investors should have been focusing on opportunities to buy future winners cheaply as the bear market dragged towards its inevitable demise, it was amazing how many were distracted by 'alternative investment strategies', lured by the promise of instant wealth for little effort. Successful investing is elusive because most investors chase the wrong priorities. Yes, success is definitely a numbers game; but not in terms of stocks bought and sold as day traders or for short-term gains. Instead, the secret lies in the number of years your money stays invested in the market. Time is the great ally for diligent stock pickers.

In August 2001, as I considered this sudden explosion of interest in 'alternative' investments, including options, derivatives, contracts for difference and spread betting, it occurred to me that investing in providers of gambling services, like investing in fund management groups, might be more profitable than joining the punters who bet on markets. Then I suddenly remembered a story from earlier in the year of a betting firm boss who donated £5 million to the Tory party for their 2001 election campaign. He became a multi-millionaire by betting against his clients, but I could not remember his name. A search of the web revealed the answer: Stuart Wheeler and his IG Group, the UK's biggest spread betting business that was listed on the London Stock Exchange in July 2000 at a price of 240p.

FASTER GAINS gets an airing

I had looked at IG Group in previous months wondering whether it was a good company to invest in. Figures early in 2001 looked promising but profits had been volatile and I remained wary. However, IG Group announced its first year of profits as a listed company on 20 July 2001. I was abroad then and did not look at its results when I came home but now I read the Annual Report on the excellent IG Group website and checked its fundamental details in *Company Refs*. Remarkably, I swiftly saw that IG Group was an almost perfect FASTER GAINS candidate and they do not crop up too often! FASTER GAINS is the stock-picking formula I developed early in the 1990s to help me find small, fast-growing companies to invest in. Eleven criteria are evaluated to cover the fundamental, technical and some general factors of a company's profile. Together, the first letter of each element forms the FASTER GAINS mnemonic, as shown in the analysis of IG Group below. But to retain that catchy phrase, the eleven factors are not presented in the order of priority, although some are clearly more important than others. Here, then is an analysis of IG Group, using my FASTER GAINS stock-picking formula to assess its virtues:

F: Fundamental facts

Although in 2001 it did not have a public five-year trading history, IG Group was founded by Stuart Wheeler in 1974. The track record since flotation showed impressive short-term growth. In an article on spread betting in the *Financial Times* on 6 October, to coincide with the introduction of new spread betting taxes, Patrick Jenkins noted, 'It is more than 25 years since IG launched as a financial spread-betting firm, but only over the past two or three years has it and its rivals begun to appeal to a mass market.' Rising interest no doubt stemmed from other betting activities, including the National Lottery, that became prominent. And once the betting genie escaped from his bottle could he be pushed back inside it again? As noted earlier, interest in spread betting was featured heavily in the financial press during the 2000–2001 economic downturn, adding to its popularity.

The company's four-year trading record revealed explosive growth: since 1998 turnover had risen 463 per cent, pre-tax profits had grown by 1,183 per cent and earnings per share had risen by 1,161 per cent, a splendid performance. Moreover, with the financial betting division doing much better than the sports division, financial spread betting could become the generator of massive growth for the group in future years as many more investors turn to spread betting as the quickest route to rapid riches. Did you know that more than 80 per cent of day traders make fast losses not quick gains? Evidence to show burgeoning popularity for spread betting was apparent in the three weeks following the September attacks on the US: rival Cantor Index announced that trading volumes had doubled during that period, with 100,000 private investors spread betting in the UK, tempted by tax breaks and the potential for big gains even during a difficult bear market. In October 2001 Stuart Wheeler, chairman and chief executive of IG Group, said: 'Times are appalling for stockbrokers, but they are very good for us.'

On 12 December 2001 *The Times* reported a mystery punter who placed one of the largest bets in the spread betting market with IG Index, part of the IG Group, hoping for a swift rise in the FTSE 100. His bet was taken out with the FTSE 100 at around 5210, with a trade equivalent to buying shares worth £20 million. On day one, the FTSE 100 was down 24 points; his loss was estimated at £196,000. On 13 December *The Times* reported his increasing loss of over £300,000 as the FTSE 100 fell another 40.8 points. The following day, with the FTSE 100 down another 45 points, this bet was looking increasingly like an impulsive error.

Although IG issued a mild profit warning in December 2001, it pointed out that it was still growing its earnings while stock-broking competitors were struggling to stay profitable. A raft of sporting events in 2002 would be beneficial to its transaction volumes, as would a stock market recovery.

Sadly, as we learned in Chapter 3, profit warnings often come in clusters, and so it proved with IG Group. In May 2002 the company announced that profits for the year would be lower than expected as cuts in their level of hedging had coincided with a greater proportion of winning bets by customers. This news, coupled with

Stuart Wheeler relinquishing his role as chief executive in March (although he remained as non-executive chairman), undermined investor confidence. The shares fell to 210p and were still languishing below the flotation price in mid-June. I decided to continue holding my shares in IG and await future developments before selling out.

A: Annual earnings per share (EPS)

For FASTER GAINS, annual earnings should reach or exceed 20 per cent. IG achieved annual earnings of 47 per cent for 2001, an impressive growth rate.

S: Supply/demand factors

There were only 54 million shares in issue, of which directors owned 34.7 per cent and major institutions 8 per cent. This left 57 per cent of shares free for trading not in the hands of long-term investors. This was a high percentage but might reduce in future as more institutions back the group.

T: Technical analysis

The price chart had only a short history but it showed the rapid surge from launch through a placing to institutional investors at 240p in July 2000 to 500p by January 2001, a rise of 108 per cent in six months. After final results were announced in July 2001, the price rose to a new high of 573p. Hitting a new high is a good sign but the forward price/earnings ratio was 22.4, rather high, and higher than Man, for example. But IG was growing at a rate far faster than 22 per cent, so I bought some shares despite the possibility of short-term falls.

E: Efficient management

Stuart Wheeler had been in the betting business for decades. In a *Financial Times* interview he confessed that once, aged seven, he spent all day studying form and turned a one shilling stake into seven shillings with two good bets on the horses. For spread betting firms, the secret of success lies in judging the odds correctly and laying off the bets, to ensure profitable results. The management team was headed by Stuart Wheeler who said he was not selling any shares even though the lock-up period was then over. This was an encouraging sign for private investors who want to back his company, as he is obviously committed to maintaining his large 32 per cent shareholding. In his interview he gave the impression of being one of those rare owners, so beloved by Warren Buffett, who show an unstinting care and commitment to running their businesses.

R: Rich in cash

Rich in cash for IG Group is the best reply to anyone who says spread betting is good for punters who take short-term bets on the market! At the year-end the cash recorded on the balance sheet was £16.5 million and the report said it had increased significantly during the year. Bets are paid for up front, boosting cash flow.

Goals are dreams with deadlines

Diana Hunt, economics writer

G: Growth in EPS

Growth in EPS should double over five years: although IG Group had a record of only four years trading as a public company, it more than amply satisfied this criterion. Growth in earnings over four years had far exceeded that doubling, rising by a massive 1,161 per cent.

A: Active monitoring

Active monitoring might prove necessary for IG Group, as it is a small company, with a market capitalisation of just £312 million. As we have seen, even with its excellent FASTER GAINS profile, things can go wrong. The new betting tax on betting shops came into operation on 1 October 2001, but IG's annual report said that even if the tax had been operating over the past year, pre-tax profits would still have exceeded 40 per cent.

There is increasing competition from smaller rivals and a number of fast-growing private firms have appeared. If they decide to float, competition could get fiercer. In the Annual Report Stuart Wheeler acknowledged additional funds will need to be spent on new technology, especially on Internet spread betting services. Finally, bookies only win if they get the odds right. One big winner can inflict heavy damage. That risk relies on clever weighing up of the odds by the management team, but a big error on hedging bets did go wrong in the spring of 2002.

I: Institutional support

Of the 54 million shares in issue the only declared institutional holding was The 140 Trustee Co. Ltd, with 8.16 per cent. As the company grows, more institutional investors could become shareholders, as future prospects seem positive. Long-term investors who climb on board before the major institutions will see their holdings rise in value as more professionals decide to back IG.

N: Something new

This criterion includes new products, or markets or a new share price high. The choices of strategy for spread betting addicts are bewilderingly huge, offering the prospects of introducing new products as opportunities arise. When I bought my holding, in two blocks during August 2001, the share price of IG Group had just hit a new high, in fact, an all-time high, from where it could fall back. I paid 577p for my shares, intending, like Stuart Wheeler and his team, to hold them long term, to let the profits grow. However, the price did fall back with the collapsing market in September 2001, and after the May 2002 profit warning, but I did not add more shares.

S: Stock market direction

As we have repeatedly noted, markets were in a steep decline, a bear phase throughout 2001. But by September, I thought we might be nearer to a revival and a turning point than to further collapse. As we have seen, the prolonged bear market did not prevent the IG share price from rising over 100 per cent from July 2000 to September 2001, and it was showing a gain of 140 per cent by August.

Having judged IG Group as a FASTER GAIN candidate we can now look briefly at its ten-bagger profile. Both formulae rely on strong fundamental facts for future prospects based on the past history, but the two approaches are slightly different. FASTER GAINS is searching for companies with strong growth potential, while the ten-bagger profile focuses more on the qualities of a visionary boss and niche leading products. *The Armchair Investor* included a FASTER GAINS profile of Sage Group, which features in my ten-bagger portfolio, and Logica was a FASTER GAINS candidate in *The Wealthy Investor*. Clearly there will be strong overlaps if we are seeking to find companies with excellent future growth prospects.

Ten-bagger profile of IG Group

Visionary chief executive with a sound business plan Stuart Wheeler had a vision of growing a successful public company and his business plan seemed well designed to produce that result.

Operates in a market with huge future growth potential In its latest financial year IG Group had produced a bumper result when all the orthodox brokerage houses were struggling. This certainly suggests that the market for betting on stocks and indices can grow even when stock markets are declining. Since the Lottery was launched Britain has become a nation of gamblers: is that likely to change? The *Financial Times* article of October 2001 noted that on some of the quiet trading days in the stock market, there had occasionally been more spread bets than share trades. According to Patrick Jenkins in the *Financial Times*, 'Whatever the moral arguments, spread betting is booming.'

Niche market with high entry costs to deter competitors Although there are numerous rivals IG Group was reckoned to have half the spread betting business, and increasing introduction of new technology investment will add to high entry costs.

Opportunity to be the leading company in its sector IG Group was already the leading company in the quoted sector. It was the UK's longest-running and largest spread betting firm.

Highly cash generative products and cash in the bank As we saw, IG Group was highly cash generative and had substantial cash reserves.

Low debt levels Debt levels were correspondingly low.

Potential to build a powerful brand IG Group had been a publicly quoted company only for less than two years, but with its large and growing client base, it could build a strong brand.

Large and expanding pool of contracts, clients, markets IG Group could expand in the UK, especially through online betting operations, and had plans to expand abroad.

Not dependent solely on one key product, market or client Conversely, these expansion plans indicate that it is not over-dependent on one product, market or group of clients.

Ability to evolve and develop new innovative products The future potential for IG Group and the whole spread betting sector looks exciting and offers excellent opportunities for introducing new products into its markets. The previous history of IG Group, extending back over a quarter of a century, indicates the positive attitude to introducing innovative products as the summary outline of its history below reveals.

The history of IG Index

1974: Founded to allow UK residents to speculate on the price of gold

1975: First bets taken

1976: Betting extended to cover all commodities traded in London

1979: IG Index bets on the movement of American markets for the first time

1981: Betting available on FTSE and Dow Jones indices, following the introduction of stock index futures in America

1993: Sports spread betting department established

1995: First bets taken on individual shares

1996: Foreign exchange dealing business started, IG's first non-betting division

1998: Internet dealings begin

1999: Margin trading on shares using contracts-for-difference (CFDs) introduced, IG's second non-betting division

2000: IG Group floats on London Stock Exchange. (IG Index is now a subsidiary of its parent company IG Group plc)

2000: IG Group won the 'New Company of the Year' award at the PLC awards sponsored by PricewaterhouseCoopers and the *Financial Times*

2001: IG Index was voted 'Best Spread Betting Firm' in the *Investors Chronicle* Investment Awards

Source: Advertising Profile of IG Index in *Investors Chronicle* Survey, Spread Betting, sponsored by IG Index, 19 October 2001

I believe in the power of the internet
and the information revolution to transform our lives
Michael Mandel, economics editor of *Business Week*

Man Group

Sector: Speciality and other finance
Market cap: £3,036 million
Share price: 1,135p
Ranking: 75
Index: FTSE 100
52-week high/low: 1,150p–599p

Forecast earnings:	P/E
2002: 55.5p	20.4
2003: 69.6p	16.3

During November 2001 Man Group, the hedge fund management group, produced very strong interim results although the stock market was struggling and most generalised fund managers were experiencing tough conditions. First half pre-tax profits grew by 154 per cent with £33.5 million generated in performance fees, well up on the £1 million in performance fees generated for 2000. I realised that Man could indeed be one of the most promising companies that I had placed on my preliminary short-list. Early in December Guardian IT produced a second profit warning for 2001, and I immediately switched my selections: I put Guardian back on the list of substitutes and Man Group on my final candidate selection. Man was heavily promoted in late October by a recommendation from Merrill Lynch with a price target of 1,350p, up from its price at that time of 1,069p. The broker repeated its 'buy' recommendation later that same week, raising its current year profit estimate from £164.5 million to £191.5 million. Reflecting strong broker support, Man's price again soared to another all-time high of 1,130p, even while the broad market was falling. Performances like this are what investors should look for.

By replacing Guardian IT with Man Group, I now have in the portfolio three companies in the Speciality and Other Finance sector. In general it would be better to have only two companies in any one sector, but this is a sample portfolio and one of my favourite choices, Vodafone, is featured separately in Chapter 10. In practice, therefore, one of the three choices in the Speciality and Other Finance sector could be changed. By replacing Guardian IT with Man Group I have increased the number of choices in the FTSE 100 index, lessening the reliance on small, higher risk choices. Guardian IT had a market value of £262 million and was a constituent of the FTSE SmallCap index, clearly making it a more risky choice than a FTSE 100 index company valued at over £3,000 million, as Man Group then was.

Vision is what they call it when others can't see what you see

Howard Schultz, founder of Starbucks coffee shop chain

Next

Sector: General retailers

Market cap: £2,876 million

Share price: 860p

Ranking: 79

Index: FTSE 100

52-week high/low: 1,012p–670p

Forecast earnings:	P/E
2002: 53.8p	16
2003: 58.6p	14.7

Next, the high street retailing giant, has been through several tough trading periods and survived every crisis. Now run by Simon Wolfson, the thirty-three-year-old son of former chairman Lord

Wolfson, he became chief executive in August 2001. Despite his youth, he already has a formidable reputation as a doyen of high fashion for the masses, with a pure marketing instinct for which new lines will sell.

Reporting on half-year results for 2001, Simon Wolfson declared that Next was already positioned in most of the retail areas it wanted to be in and predicted that growth would come from moving shops to bigger sites or extending existing premises. He said: 'We have stores in the majority of towns and cities that can profitably sustain a Next store.' Group sales had grown to £794 million, up from £685 million, and sales of men's suits were strong, while pre-tax profits for the first six months of the year had risen from £80.7 million to £93 million. Over the past twelve months Next had expanded its selling space by 328,000 square feet, after opening thirteen sites previously owned by C&A, the retailer that withdrew from the UK early in 2001.

While many retailers were struggling, Next had captured many dissatisfied Marks & Spencer customers, but experts were rating it as a good business in its own right, with plans to boost sales through opening new stores. The management team proved skilful at anticipating fashion trends. By positioning itself at the top end of the mass market Next had avoided competition with the value and discount stores, one of the few UK retailers that managed to increase its market share consistently.

Is Next a future ten-bagger? In mid-1997 the premier flagship retailer was undoubtedly Marks & Spencer, ranked 11 in the FTSE 100 index, while Next was ranked at 85 and valued at £2,653 million. Over the intervening four years Marks & Spencer had collapsed to a position of 43rd and while Next appeared to have made little progress, moving from 85th place to 79th, it may yet be capable of growing to fill the gap at the apex of the FTSE 100 index vacated by Marks & Spencer.

Ryanair

Sector: Transport
Market cap: £2,303 million
Share price: 318p
Ranking: 94
Index: Not included in any UK Index as it is based in Ireland
52-week high/low: 410.5p–225p

Forecast earnings:	P/E
2002: 0.185p	17.2
2003: 0.23p	13.8

In December 2001, Ryanair made a share split: each share was divided into two. The revised price after December was subsequently the equivalent of 318p. The earnings figures have also been adjusted for the share split.

Ryanair, Europe's largest low-cost airline in 2001, was a novel trendsetter in the difficult airline industry, being among the first to build and operate a low fares business plan. It set new records for fast growth in this mature, intensely competitive and cyclical sector. Air travel is one of the most volatile and cyclical market sectors and national flag carriers get support from their domestic governments. Despite deregulation in the industry subsidies from national governments merely aggravated overcapacity, creating serious difficulties for almost every airline. Being cyclical poses perennial problems: when the economy booms, more people travel on business and for pleasure. During recessions, demand falls and airlines struggle to make profits. Negative market conditions during the autumn of 2001, especially after the September terror attacks on America, illustrate the problems: rising expenses are coupled with falling revenues and declining demand.

Facing such turbulent conditions, most European airlines, both for regular flights and some low-cost routes, issued profit warnings, reported losses and large job cuts, while vociferously seeking grants and financial support from national governments. Yet despite so much misery, Ryanair continued to deliver growth in its fleet, new routes, traffic, revenues and profitability.

Because low-cost carriers operate only as point-to-point airlines inside Europe, they avoided the major disruptions to transatlantic and long haul flights following the 11 September terrorist attacks on America. Michael O'Leary, Ryanair's chief executive explained, 'We have no connecting traffic and are not directly exposed to any downturn in such traffic, either on transatlantic routes or at hub airports.' The majority of seats were already being sold through the Internet, another factor that helped to reduce costs, although prices excluded taxes and airport charges. Selling extra services, such as hotel and car hire bookings boosted revenues.

A week after terrorists destroyed the World Trade Center in New York, Michael O'Leary claimed that prospects had not been harmed. Bookings for flights to Europe were back to 90 per cent of their levels before the attack. In response to the 11 September events, Ryanair and its rival budget airlines immediately introduced a series of promotions for seat sales and special offers to tempt traffic back. It reduced advance booking periods for the cheap fares on many flights to stimulate sales and hoped to contain the damage to fare yields by continuing to sell part of its capacity at higher prices to late bookers. According to Ray Webster, chief executive of EasyJet: 'The imperative was to get people travelling again. You can't make margins unless you get people to take the product.'

The growing popularity of the low-cost budget airlines and caution for long-haul carriers were built on the belief that the low-cost group – Ryanair, EasyJet, Buzz and Go – could benefit from the crisis by accelerating their planned expansion of capacity and taking advantage of sweeping cutbacks imposed by traditional carriers. Tim Jeans, Ryanair's marketing director, thought a larger gap would arise between the full service and low-cost carriers. Ryanair hoped to benefit from an expected fall in prices of new and second-hand aircraft, planning to acquire up to fifty aircraft to maintain its growth beyond 2003.

In June 2002 Ryanair decisively silenced its critics by announcing stellar full year results: record profits of €172 million (£111 million), passenger numbers up 38 per cent to 11.1 million in 2001 and forecast to grow 35 per cent in 2002, and average ticket prices reduced by 8 per cent. Margins climbed to 24 per cent as the focus stayed resolutely on driving down costs. The shares rose on this news but some influential journalists (the *Financial Times* Lex column and Tempus in *The Times*) still rated them 'a buy'.

Luck occurs when opportunity meets preparation
Arno Penzias, entrepreneur

Sage Group

Sector: Software and computer services
Market cap: £2,704 million
Share price: 213p
Ranking: 82
Index: FTSE 100
52-week high/low: 381p–149p

Forecast earnings:	P/E
2002: 7.68	27.7
2003: 8.8p (assumes 15 per cent increase)	24.2

I have had a long relationship with Sage Group, which featured in my portfolio on three separate occasions and was analysed in detail in Chapter 9 of *The Armchair Investor*, published by Orion. Not only was Sage Group the best performing share of the 1990s, it fulfilled two of the legendary Peter Lynch's criteria for winning companies: first it was a ten-bagger several times over during its first ten years as a quoted company, and, second, its core business is accounting software packages, which most people find boring. But boring certainly did not describe its spectacular share price performance! The chief architect of Sage's early success was David Goldman, but chief executive Paul Walker has been driving growth forward since 1994. On 8 November 1999 he said: 'When you look at Sage compared with other IT companies, as we start the year our revenues are predictable because they come from our user base.' Few software companies could boast such a sound track record. In 2000 pre-tax profits grew 47 per cent to £109 million although trading conditions were difficult and many firms were struggling. Since 1997 sales of its software accounting packages to small and medium-sized firms had quadrupled to £412 million. Part of its strength stemmed from recurring sales to existing clients; by 2001 this was around two-thirds of sales including sales of new products.

I knew the more I understood about the company, the better off I would be

Benjamin Graham, founding father of company fundamental analysis, author of *The Intelligent Investor*

In the turbulent IT world Sage was a rare phenomenon: while most companies remain notoriously cyclical, Sage had unique defensive qualities, deriving two-thirds of its revenues from an army of 2.7 million small and medium-sized firms, a formidable client base. Customers paid regular sums for support services, specialised stationery and customer relationship management (CRM) software, providing Sage with reliable relatively secure revenues.

After the June 2002 FTSE 100 review, Sage was the only pure technology company left in the index, as ARM Holdings and Logica were both relegated.

Acquisitions played a major role in Sage's successful expansion:

from 1992 at least one new business was added each year. American acquisitions gave it a huge footprint in this highly technology-oriented economy. Unlike hundreds of UK companies, Sage was able to integrate all its acquisitions successfully, including, most remarkably, US takeovers, where many major UK companies (including Marks & Spencer and Stagecoach, the transport group) floundered publicly over misadventures.

In typical fashion, during the best time for stock holding, people were the most reluctant to hold them.
John Rothchild, author of *The Davis Dynasty*, 2001

How long can Sage continue to expand at rates exceeding 25 per cent a year? Although it is far from reaching saturation point, growth in its core small and medium-sized applications market might slow, putting pressure on the newly installed Internet operations. In 2001 Microsoft bought major rival Great Plains, intensifying threats from larger US competitors.

To be a ten-bagger from late September 2001, Sage must grow its share price from 155p to 1,550p. On a forward multiple of 55, earnings would have to reach around 28p; a tall order, but not altogether impossible by 2011.

If you see a bandwagon, it's too late
Sir James Goldsmith, financier and entrepreneur

Work to a system

As Philip Fisher, the celebrated US fund manager observed, great stocks are extremely difficult to find. This is why working to a system gives investors an edge: it provides essential discipline to ensure you stay faithful to your potential ten-baggers, once you have been smart enough to find them. The ten-bagger profile pinpoints possible winners, but buying them at inflated prices is counterproductive, reducing their potential at the outset.

Preparing a suitable buy plan is therefore a vital step to avoid simply drifting into owning a portfolio of hopefuls. Tilt the odds towards winning with a carefully planned and executed buy programme, described in the next chapter.

8 **Buying Routines**

We know that there are no limits to what can be achieved with will, vision and determination. And we have all three in abundance

Jorma Ollila, CEO of Nokia

If you plan to hold your shares for ten years, short-term volatility will not matter too much, except at the outset when you buy your holdings. If you acquire them in a depressed market you stand a far higher chance of achieving ten-bagger returns because it is naturally easier for a share price to double many times over from a low start.

Catching the market's moods

Investment is not rocket science, relying more on experience learned in the rough and tumble of the hectic marketplace. Over the course of 2001 markets were exceptionally volatile with a continuous onslaught of dire news. Was this the time to buy? Should we be selling, or waiting until the outlook cleared? Fundamental analysis is excellent for examining company health but does not offer a complete guide for some of these tough issues.

Although investors must study the fundamental features of companies they plan to buy shares in, plenty of useful information is buried in the charts of share prices and the benchmark indices for large exchanges, such as the UK's FTSE 100 and the US Dow Jones Industrial Average. Technical analysis is the study of a wide range of technical factors that cover market behaviour; the regular use of such factors sheds light on how the market is behaving now in the context of earlier behaviour. One of the most widely used technical tools is the examination of charts.

I have always thought powerful influences drive human behaviour, which sometimes seems irrational, especially in stock markets. Benjamin Graham, father of fundamental analysis, described the market as 'manic depressive': excessive euphoria one day was followed by deep depression the next. Technical analysis with a wide array of market indicators is precisely designed to study this aspect of the market's performance. Its range of indicators examines the collective psychology of investors when they act en masse, to assess what is going on now and what conclusions can perhaps be drawn from their past behaviour.

However, a large army of sceptics views charts and technical indicators as mumbo-jumbo. This antagonism is excellent news as it means they disregard this whole area of analysis. Irrational market behaviour is ubiquitous. Sceptical investors who ignore it, by discrediting technical analysis tools specifically designed to study mass behaviour by market participants, make successful investing even tougher than it already is. For those of us willing to examine the technical indicators, the fewer people there are who study the markets' complex movements, the better the prospects for large gains, because we know the majority of investors are always wrong. Stay with the minority to benefit from the winning strategy.

Oddly, one endorsement for technical analysis comes from the famous Coppock indicator, described by Edwin Coppock. Although its origins are firmly grounded in human psychology, it is apparently followed by numerous market-watchers, including some opponents of technical analysis. The indicator gives guidance on a revival of optimism during a bear market, based on the psychology of bereavement. In 1962 Edwin Coppock devised an ingenious test based on people's reactions to a severe bereavement to find the low point in a bear market. Priests at a local church told him that it takes mourners between eleven to fourteen months to adjust to the death of a close relative. Although a massive loss in wealth may not directly equate to the loss of a much-loved family member, the Coppock indicator is based on the quite natural implication that investors who have suffered severe losses during a financial bubble or stock market crash will need time to recover their buying enthusiasm after a period of market turbulence. Accordingly, the indicator Edwin Coppock devised is based on assessing the level of optimism or despair among the whole class of investors as measured by main benchmark indices, such as the FTSE 100 index. Encouragingly, this indicator has given some very reliable 'buy' signals but also a few false alarms. It is surprisingly successful in alerting investors to a change of mood, especially at a low point, when it signals a 'buy'. For ten-bagger hunters planning to stay invested for several years, it is comforting to know that the 'buy' signals have proved more reliable than the 'sell' signals.

The indicator compares the value of an index at the end of a month with its level eleven and fourteen months previously, using a weighted average. Although the calculation is complicated, the chart and the signal it produces are not. What is significant, according to Edwin Coppock, is when the numbers start rising while they are still negative, indicating a subtle change of mood at a market bottom. This generates the 'buy' signal. Official Coppock 'buy' signals are rare events but one was signalled for the technology-heavy American Nasdaq Composite, and also for the UK FTSE techMARK 100 index at the end of November 2001. UK technology shares tend to closely mirror the behaviour of the American technology sector, so it was doubly reassuring to see a 'buy' signal for both these indices. The chart on page 142 appeared in the *Investors Chronicle* early in December, as the magazine calculates the situation for the indicator for a wide range of different stock markets at the end of every month.

The chart shows two lines: the price line for the FTSE techMARK

FTSE techMARK 100 and Coppock Indicator

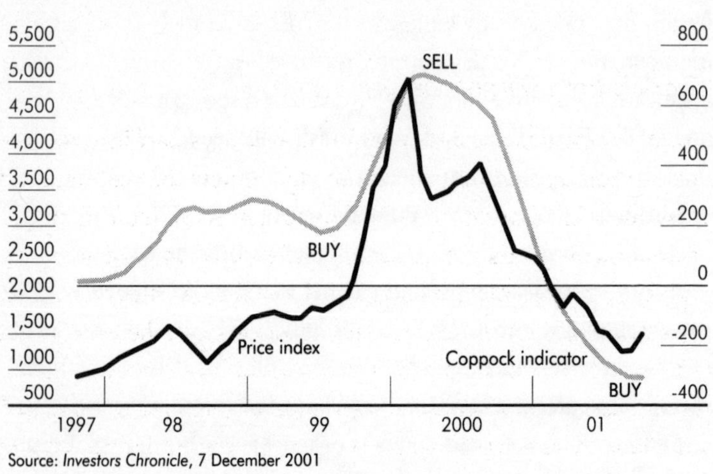

Source: *Investors Chronicle*, 7 December 2001

100 index and the line of the Coppock Indicator. Note the unofficial 'buy' signal in autumn 1999 (unofficial because the line was not in negative territory), the 'sell' signal in January 2000 and the official 'buy' signal in November 2001. This proved to be a premature signal, however, as the FTSE techMARK went on to record all-time lows in May and June 2002.

Technical analysis is a complement to a fundamental examination and its principal role is to reveal a series of subtle clues about what is going on. The more each clue enforces other clues, the more reliable the insight. Indeed, anyone who followed market events over the summer and autumn of 2001 and did not spot the despair and despondency that drove prices to three-year lows should probably not be investing in equities at all.

Investors who follow the charts plus some of the simpler technical indicators will gain a deeper insight into what is underway than if these useful signals are ignored entirely.

Nothing energises traders like the smell of Greenbacks
Rory Godson, *Sunday Times*

Signals from winners or losers

Months before the economy begins to recover, smart investors are on the scent, based on their knowledge of how the economy will react in a few months' time. If central bankers inject a monetary stimulus, investors anticipate a rally and embark on an early buying spree. A number of technical statistics will reveal the increase in buying activity: for example, a massive increase in the numbers of shares traded on a daily basis; a rise in the closely followed benchmark FTSE 100 index; larger numbers of rising as compared to falling share prices on any particular day and widespread rising share prices. If you spot some of these indicators you can begin to quantify mounting optimism. Conversely, when investors are worried, the majority grow pessimistic and sell shares in great volumes. Important technical signals, including a steeply falling benchmark index, volumes of shares traded, numbers of share prices falling and declining prices, will register this collective mood as investors sell en masse. Even when markets are drifting with no obvious trend, technical analysts glean useful signals as drifting implies investor uncertainty. During December 2001, for example, the FTSE 100 index rose strongly to approach 5400 before subsiding rapidly back to below 5050, a level it had last seen during October. Was it going to move lower still or recover again? The economic signals were mixed, implying there was no clear direction for the market. Drifting markets denote ambiguity as investors are unsure which way they will move next. In such situations, cautious investors should watch and wait for a clearer signal to emerge, although it is possible some of your target buy prices might crop up during an uncertain phase.

Checking the charts

Studying the charts is one of the great benefits of technical analysis; it is an excellent tool for investors who want to find particular price levels where previous support or resistance was evident in a share price or index. I covered the whole topic of technical analysis in *The Armchair Investor*, as it is the T-factor in FASTER GAINS. Readers of *Backing Winners* should use technical analysis for valuable buy or sell signals that might appear on any trading day. These signals offer useful clues together with numbers of shares traded, new highs in a share price or sudden breakouts, either up or down. Top of the list for information is regular examination of share price or index charts to find those elusive support or resistance levels. They indicate prices where, collectively, investors might again begin buying after a fall (support emerges) or selling after a rise (meaning that resistance has returned at this particular price).

This behaviour was notable for ARM Holdings where the share price failed on three separate occasions in April and May 2001 to push up above 400p. The price dropped back to 200p in June and July and revisited that lower (support) level again on three further occasions. When the price fell to 197p during the morning of 21 September 2001, amid a market panic, I added to my holding. During 2001 Capita Group managed to maintain a trading range between 400p and 520p. Every time the price hit 400p buyers appeared (bringing support) but when it rose above 500p sellers emerged (illustrating renewed resistance above that level).

Several companies feature updated share price charts on their own websites, while several websites cover charts. I use BigCharts, whose URL is http://bigcharts.marketwatch.com for tracking shares I am following, but http://stockcharts.com is a good alternative: it has comprehensive technical analysis plus some interesting educational features.

Luck is the opportunity you take when it presents itself
Hasim Rahman, boxer, after he knocked out champion Lennox Lewis

Setting buy prices

Arriving at a sensible buying price begins with fundamental analysis. Then, having set a target price, examine the chart to detect support or resistance levels. Are they above or below the price you decided upon by examining price/earnings ratios? When support levels appear on a chart they give some guidance on how over- or undervalued a company is before you buy shares, as we will see shortly with ARM Holdings. Prices are relative, however, depending on how popular a company is and its current reputation for growth. Fast-growing companies trade at high price/earnings ratios because they are rare and investors hope the growth will continue. If it does, the price/earnings ratio will fall over a few years. I bought Logica shares at 230p in 1997 when earnings were 5.81p. The price/earnings ratio on my purchase was 39.6 (230 ÷ 5.81): in 2001 earnings were 25.1p, reducing the price/earnings ratio to 9.2 (230 ÷ 25.1) *Company Refs* shows average forecast earnings of 29.5p for 2002 and 34.3 for 2003, on low growth rates of around 16 per cent. If the low earnings forecasts are met, the price/earnings ratio on my shares falls to 7.8 for 2002 and 6.7 for 2003. This dramatic fall in price/earnings ratios depends on two exceptional factors: first, Logica must grow its earnings strongly every year and second, I must continue to hold my shares. Sadly, neither of these factors materialised with my Logica holdings during 2002.

We can compare this steep decline in price/earnings figures for my Logica and Sage Group holdings. I bought Sage in 1999 at 251p and paid a hefty price/earnings ratio of 59 as earnings were 4.25p; by 2000 earnings had risen to 5.78p dropping the price/earnings ratio to 43, still high. *Company Refs* gives forecast earnings of 7.68p for 2002. If those earnings do materialise, the price/earnings ratio on my initial purchase would fall to 32.6.

Looking to the future, we can examine prospects for ARM Holdings, another company in the sample ten-bagger portfolio, to judge price/earnings, sensible buy prices and how they relate to chart price levels. November's *Company Refs* had an average broker forecast of earnings of 3.38p for 2001 and 4.35p for 2002. On 13 November at a price of 390p, ARM's price/earnings ratio was 115 for 2001 (390p ÷ 3.38p) and 89.7 for 2002 (390p ÷ 4.35p), revealing how much future growth was already factored in, although investors and analysts were encouraged by excellent October third quarter results. Back on 1 October, at a price of 225p, the price/earnings ratio for 2001 was much lower at 66.5 (225p ÷ 3.38p) and 51.7 for 2002. These ratios are very high, but what does the chart show?

As earlier noted, a price chart of ARM Holdings reveals support at 200p on several occasions; first during June, July and August 1999, when it stayed in a tight trading range around 200p for about three months. After a huge surge to 1,000p in the spring of 2000, it declined to hit 200p again in mid-July 2001. It then rose to 300p before falling back again during September. The 11 September terrorist attacks weakened market sentiment severely. On 21 September prices plunged during a global panic; ARM's price fell to around 196p twice during the morning and I bought shares at 197p on the second occasion, for an average price of 199.5p with costs added. At 200p the price/earnings ratio fell to 59 for 2001 and 46 for 2002. This is still a high valuation, but at least I had avoided buying at a price/earnings ratio exceeding 100.

Prepare your buying plan

As earlier discussed, a ten-bagger portfolio needs around ten candidates as you limit the chances of success by holding too few companies. Having established a preliminary short list over several months and whittled it down to ten favourites, it is time to prepare your buying plan. Find a sensible buy price from the earnings and p/e record, and check chart patterns to decide on a feasible price. Follow the market to catch any opportunities to buy at that price. Buy your ten over a period of six months to one year, depending on the background market conditions and whether your target buy prices emerge. Be ready to adjust the target buy prices if markets undergo sudden moves. The routine steps for preparing your buy plan are set out in the table below.

Prepare a buying plan

1. Follow the progress of your preliminary short-list companies
2. Whittle down fifteen to twenty companies to ten, spread over seven or eight sectors
3. Prepare your buying plan
4. Check the current and forecast earnings record
5. Use a reasonable price/earnings ratio to set a buy price
6. Check the chart patterns on each choice to test your target buy prices
7. Follow the market to catch the opportunities to buy at the prices you have set
8. Buy the ten selected companies over a period of six months to one year, depending on market conditions and whether your target buy prices crop up
9. Be ready to adjust target buy prices if markets move abruptly
10. If target buy prices are elusive, buy your holding in two separate blocks

Expose yourself to the best things humans have done and then try to bring those things into what you are doing

Steve Jobs, co-founder of Apple Computer

Hitting a moving target

If you intend to spend £1,000 per holding, the more shares it can buy, the better the chances of higher returns, although shares must never be bought simply because they are cheap. There could be serious reasons for low prices. A share is only a bargain if its underlying value is roughly equal to the price you pay. Companies experiencing trading problems or financial weaknesses will seldom be future ten-baggers, but by following a company you think has great promise you might be able to buy shares cheaply on days when the whole market is falling as we saw with my purchase of ARM. Buying on weakness is possible only by tracking shares over several weeks or months. Even then, your target prices may not appear.

As with buying new furniture at a summer discount, it makes sense to try to buy your chosen shares at bargain prices from where it is easier to double or treble your funds. You also buy more shares and thereby gain an extra dividend for each added share (in 2001 ARM paid no dividends, but it did have a fantastic growth record to compensate). The more shares you own the larger will be your dividend income and then the more shares that cash can buy next year if you reinvest your dividends. So buying cheaply starts a virtuous circle, which over time can make a significant difference to the ultimate strength and size of your portfolio. However, it is extremely difficult to buy shares at target prices as they continuously change in the large, liquid FTSE 100 and 250 stocks: you are inevitably shooting at a moving target. Smaller companies, by contrast, show modest daily trading. Prices may stay flat for weeks or possibly months. This is advantageous if the price is at the level you have chosen, but if not, prolonged periods of static prices mean waiting weeks before the chosen price crops up.

I saw this outcome most frustratingly with my Capita Group holdings; I followed the price for weeks. I lost patience and bought shares at 500p in summer 2001 only to see the price collapse with the continuing retreat of the main market through the early autumn. With IG Group, I bought at a share price high of 575p, hoping the shares would continue rising as they were trading at a price/earnings ratio of around 21. During September, as prices fell, I knew if I had been patient I could have bought them more cheaply. We need to be flexible when setting target buy prices; if we finally have to pay more than we estimated, this may not be a disaster if the plan is to hold shares for at least ten years.

Organising the buying plan

If you plan to buy shares in companies with high price volatility, such as ARM Holdings or Vodafone, try a routine I frequently use when future market moves look uncertain. Buy your holding in two separate blocks, investing the first £500 at 150p followed by the second £500 at 135p if that price fall occurs within weeks. When target buy prices prove elusive a change of strategy may be needed. Every investor will judge the future tactics for the buying plan and reassess chosen target prices to benefit from market changes as they unfold.

For example, I wanted to add more IG Group to hold outside my Personal Equity Plan (Pep), as I like obtaining information directly from the company. I decided to buy more IG shares if the price rose above its previous all-time high, setting a target price of 578p. This move is known in technical jargon as a 'breakout on the upside'. Once a share manages to move above a previous high, it can sometimes soar quickly to a new high, which explains the term 'breakout'. I was hoping IG Group could achieve this after the change in betting taxes introduced on 1 October 2001, as this seemed positively to encourage gambling.

Adding to a holding like this is called pyramiding: you buy more shares when the price breaks out upwards to a new high level. I did this with IG Group during October, buying my shares on a day the market was falling steeply but IG Group rose to a new all-time high of 578p. I saw this as positive for further rises. However, the markets remained sensitive to continuing bad news so the hoped-for IG breakout was feeble, reaching only 595p on 13 November. Strong breakouts on the upside occur more often during bull markets. It is probably too much to expect a robust surge when the markets are persistently pessimistic.

Setting target buy prices is more of an art than a science. However, the long-term buy-and-hold strategy does give investors some latitude. If a share is going to rise from 160p to 1,600p over ten years, buying at 165p or even 170p may raise the ten-bagger target, but this will not destroy the concept of achieving fantastic gains, if a result anywhere close was ultimately reached. Moreover, buying shareholdings is not an exercise set in stone; some flexibility is sensible.

After the ten-bagger portfolio is up and running, how you decide to track its progress may make a significant difference to the eventual outcome. Tracking the portfolio is therefore extremely important, a topic discussed in Chapter 9.

Success = Ability × Effort × Attitude

Kazuo Inamori, founder of Kyocera Corporation and KDDI Corporation, both Japanese telephone companies

9 Keep Tracking

There is virtually no kind of situation that can't be handled with a system

Robert R. Godfrey, economics writer

Although most financial observers are pessimistic about future returns, investors should not be downcast: we have seen that numerous strategies can tilt the odds towards success. By focusing on the winning strategies we can improve our chances of securing good returns. *Backing Winners* is an investment system that focuses on these winning strategies using a four-pronged approach: first, uncover promising ten-bagger companies; second, use a disciplined formula to avoid buying losers or sell them before they cripple portfolio performance; third, apply sensible routines to tilt the odds towards winning, especially with target buy prices; and fourth, adopt a sensible tracking routine. This is the final prong and the main topic for this chapter.

'New' attitudes for 'old'

Warren Buffett suggests we view ourselves as part-owners in companies we choose to invest in. This requires a totally different attitude to our portfolios: instead of holding a random cluster of shares in UK companies, we should regard ourselves as owners of companies whose shares we buy, confident that they will be successful long-term investments. This constructive attitude applies to all investors, as it colours your whole approach to future investment decisions. A ten-bagger company in your portfolio is not just a 'share' for trading; it is part of your current wealth. Its fortunes will be as close to your interests as events that damage or enhance the area where you live or the house you are buying on a long-term mortgage.

Essentially, there are three separate tracking options: once the portfolio is established you can leave it on automatic pilot for years ahead. Alternatively, by putting in some time and effort, you could check its progress with an annual review. The third, most active option involves following the fortunes of your chosen ten, selling losers as any unfavourable warning signs appear and reinvesting these proceeds in new or existing winners. We will look at these three options in turn.

Follow a tracking option

1. 'Automatic pilot' – completely hands-off for about ten years
2. 'Lazy tracking' – perform a regular yearly review
3. 'Busy tracking' – actively sell losers as necessary, to reinvest in winners

'Automatic pilot' option

Logically, it seems self-evident that a proven strategy will include backing winners and evicting losers, but how will you discover which ten-bagger hopefuls become losers if you leave your new portfolio on automatic pilot and rarely give it a second glance, for several years? While this option looks like a complete recipe for disaster, it can still prove highly successful, especially if you initially devoted plenty of time and effort to choosing your most promising ten-bagger companies. You might decide to regard setting up the ten-bagger portfolio as the most important part of the Ten-point Action Plan, taking time to find and buy ten convincing candidates at moderate prices. What result can you expect if you then decide to sit back and leave the portfolio simmering while you go off and enjoy life to the full over ten years? I believe the results can be exciting, if your choice does indeed include some potential ten-baggers; the profits should, in theory, take care of themselves. There is good evidence to suggest investors who are smart stock pickers can produce a great performance with a completely hands-off tracking system, as I illustrated in my book *The Wealthy Investor*. A ten-year portfolio of the top ten FTSE 100 companies in mid-1988, held passively to mid-1998 grew from £10,000 to over £60,000 without including reinvested dividends. It contained only one ten-bagger: the investment in drugs firm Glaxo grew from £1,000 to £10,000 over the ten years. I should point out that timing played a positive part in this result as 1988 was the year following the October 1987 crash and most investors were too shell-shocked to be buying shares, while mid-1998 was a market high. Encouragingly, therefore, setting up a ten-bagger portfolio during 2002–3 should offer good timing, as the markets were caught in a prolonged bear phase during 2001–2.

Indeed, a healthy long-term lethargy will also protect your portfolio from misplaced activity when you might inadvertently sell ten-bagger candidates prematurely before they have had sufficient time to fulfil their true long-term potential. Lethargy can be an investor's best friend. Some activity might even accentuate the losses rather than correct an already poor performance. Consider the sorry fate that befell former England rugby player Andy Ripley, featured in *The Times* on 19 October 2001. He sold his shares in Marconi, the debt-laden telecommunications equipment company, to buy 25,000 Railtrack shares at 280p on the morning of 5 October, just a few hours before the government put the rail infrastructure company into administration and suspended the shares. To add more agony to his lost £70,000, reputedly his life's savings, between 5 and 19 October Marconi shares had recovered from their panic lows and had tripled in value from the time of his sale. If he had simply continued holding them his stake would have grown to £210,000 by 19 October without doing anything. This is a sobering reflection on the hazards investors might face by jumping out of one losing investment and into another.

Investors might occasionally read about their companies while taking no further interventionist actions. However, as reinvesting your annual dividends can transform a portfolio, investigate whether the registrars dealing with your companies run dividend reinvestment schemes, which many do. If so, even that element of improving your portfolio performance will be automatically catered for.

> *To be truly successful and achieve great results*
> *we must first fall in love with our work*
>
> Kazuo Inamori, founder of Kyocera Corporation and KDDI Corporation

'Lazy tracking' option

Leaving the whole enterprise to chance might work, but one of the other two tracking options should prove more successful.

Both lazy and busy trackers should compile scrapbooks or files of press cuttings on companies and items of information picked up during reading. File everything in a personal organiser, a filing cabinet, on your PC or, best of all, try to keep the most important details in your personal memory bank, which is why investors should focus on owning shares in a maximum of only ten companies. Compile an organised database of information, so that you can find important news items about your companies quickly, if needed.

As we saw in Chapter 4 Tilting the Odds, investors tend to make several common mistakes, but even if faulty investment habits have knocked your performance, you can claw back ground through an annual portfolio review to remove outright losers and reinvest in existing winners.

Perform an annual review

To conduct an annual review, collect the routine information companies send out to all investors every year: annual and interim reports, information on a rights issue or on other key events. Try to attend the Annual General Meetings of your companies, as this offers an important opportunity to meet the directors and ask questions. If you are too shy to ask a question another shareholder might ask it during the meeting. Unfortunately, many companies are based widely around Britain; I would have to travel to Cambridge for the ARM Holdings AGM, Edinburgh for Royal Bank of Scotland, Newcastle for Sage Group and Rainham, Essex, for Carpetright, all hours away from my home. Once a year, calculate the value of your entire portfolio by revaluing each company at the day's closing price. Then compare the value of each holding in percentage terms with the initial purchase price you paid. Incidentally, while you are compiling the annual review, why not do a complete wealth check by adding up the value of all your assets, house, pension, bank deposits, shareholdings, including the ten-bagger portfolio and deducting all your debts? This is an excellent way to track how your wealth is growing.

On the first anniversary this is an information-only exercise, especially for the ten-bagger portfolio, but at the end of year 2, when you do the next portfolio valuation, you can begin to make meaningful comparisons among your ten companies. The stages of the annual review are itemised below.

Annual review procedures

1 Collect annual reports from the company or its website
2 Read what the chairman has to say and the financial highlights
3 Try to attend the Annual General Meeting each year, if possible
4 Calculate the value of each company in the portfolio
5 Compare the value of each holding, in percentage terms, with the initial purchase price

6 Grade the companies in order of performance, with the worst performers at the top of the list, ready to review the overall performance in one year's time
7 Compile a list of all your assets, including the ten-bagger portfolio
8 Compile a list of all your debts and loans
9 Deduct the total debts from your total assets to arrive at your NET WEALTH
10 Repeat the whole exercise around the same date every year

Below is a sample portfolio to show the valuation process. This portfolio is compiled from some companies in the preliminary short-list that existed in January 2000 but were not in the sample portfolio of Chapter 7 The Ten-bagger Portfolio plus seven other major companies chosen at random: Bank of Scotland (now merged with Halifax), Border TV, EMI (the record group), Manchester United Football Club, retailer W. H. Smith, Vodafone (featured in Chapter 10) and WPP (the global advertising firm). The number of shares in each bought for £1,000 was rounded down to the next whole number, after deducting £25 for costs. This is a rough guide because dividing £975 by the cost of highly priced shares leaves a larger cash remnant than for cheaper shares. The valuations shown cover the year 2 January 2000 to 2 January 2001.

Sample portfolio valuations at Annual Review – 2 January 2001

No of shares	*Company*	*Price*	*Value 2.1.00*	*Price*	*Value 2.1.01*	*Percentage rise/fall*
135	Bank of Scotland	719p	£970	701p	£946	-2.5%
126	Border TV	773p	£974	1,450p	£1,827	+88%
183	Celltech	532p	£973	1,183p	£2,165	+122.5%
160	EMI Group	608p	£973	550p	£880	-10%
236	Man Group	413p	£974	616p	£1,454	+49%
475	Manchester United	205p	£973	224p	£1,064	+9.4%

224	Phytopharm	435p	£974	850p	£1,904	+95%
468	Smith & Nephew	208p	£973	310p	£1,451	+49%
317	Vodafone	307p	£973	246p	£779	-20%
203	WHSmith	480p	£974	426p	£865	-11%

Having prepared the portfolio valuation, you can now assess any possible laggards, by grading the ten companies according to the percentage losses/gains shown. Begin by putting the companies showing the largest losses at the top of the list. These may soon need a decision on whether to sell or to continue to hold them in the portfolio. By repeating the annual review on the same day each year, you keep track of your progress.

Portfolio rearranged in order of losses/gains

Company	*Loss/Gain*	*Comment*
Vodafone	-20%	Needs a longer time frame for 3G services to arrive
WHSmith	-11%	Are managers tackling the problems?
EMI Group	-10%	Is a takeover or merger likely?
Bank of Scotland	-2.5%	Will the merger with Halifax improve profitability?
Man United	+9.4%	Is this still a good long-term investment?
Man Group	+49%	Can growth continue at this pace?
Smith & Nephew*	+49%	Was this rise due to investor over-exuberance?
Phytopharm*	+95%	Can this company develop ten-bagger products?
Celltech*	+122.5%	Is the share price running ahead of events?

* Pharmaceuticals or healthcare company.

Victory never comes to those who fear losing it
Juan Fangio, Argentinian racing driver

Valuation posers

During 2000 global stock markets were still enjoying the last phase of the great millennium boom. Vodafone was rising towards a high of 399p, the leading group in the still fashionable mobile telecom sector, while biotechnology companies were storming higher. Note that this sample portfolio included a pharmaceutical company, a healthcare group and an innovative drugs company (marked *), all of whom produced impressive rises, but three health-related companies in one portfolio is risky: they could have produced hefty losses!

As 2000 produced some excellent returns for several companies, this portfolio could simply stand as it is for a second year. The next annual review would be on 2 January 2002; if Vodafone and W. H. Smith were still showing disappointing performances, then a reassessment of the long-term potentials could be undertaken to decide whether to hold for another year, or sell. Assessing future ten-bagger prospects while the portfolio is running is one vital aspect of improving returns. When rival companies report bad news, investors should be vigilant about a company's ability to avoid similar problems. Then if unexpected adversity is announced investors would be prepared and can swiftly reach a selling decision.

But investors who opt for lazy tracking do face a problem: the opportunity to intervene between two annual review dates might prevent rescuing the portfolio from a dreadful collapse, as occurred at Marconi and Independent Insurance among others during 2001.

Investors in Marconi who did an annual review on 1 November 2001 might find in retrospect that they had locked themselves into a failed company. They would then discover that the value of the

Marconi holding was down to perhaps £97.50 at a price of 30p, if 325 shares had initially been bought at 300p each in November 2000, a shocking result. To avoid such miserable outcomes, lazy trackers might decide to become busy during an economic downturn. They might then join with investors who take the busy tracking option and use a more interventionist approach to avoid a corporate crisis. This approach might have generated an early sell signal for Marconi, as brokers, analysts and even some influential journalists in the financial press were recommending a 'sell' in July and August.

For investors who remain on board, watching an alarming share price collapse and uncertain when or whether to sell as bad news continues to flow, various signs appear to help in making a decision. Comments and interviews in the financial press give some guidance, as do live TV interviews on financial programmes. When newly appointed executives are installed to clear up a previous financial mess, as at Marconi and Baltimore Technologies, investors should try to evaluate their recovery plans. We saw that Bijan Khezri at Baltimore Technologies adopted a realistic approach to the huge tasks he faced, admitting Baltimore had pursued flawed policies. He outlined his key objectives to reassure investors. His task posed huge challenges, but such interviews might help uncertain shareholders form a rational approach to recovery potentials. Investors could compile a chronicle of events charting the growing problems, as outlined in Chapter 3 for Independent Insurance and Marconi. The table below gives a sample of key questions shareholders might consider when deciding whether to sell or hold for another few months before reviewing the situation again. Sadly, a failed company with massive problems might take years to turn around, just look at how long it required to make improvements in the performance of retailing giants such as Sainsbury and Marks & Spencer. Recovery prospects should receive six-monthly checks to ensure the situation remains stable, or is improving. If faced with a further deterioration, repeat the quiz to decide once again whether a troublesome investment should be sold or held for another six months.

I have an edge because a lot of people I compete with are not looking for reasons to buy. They are looking for reasons not to buy

Peter Lynch, manager of Fidelity's Magellan Fund, 1977 to 1990

Deciding whether to sell shares in a crisis company

1. Has the company installed new managers who recognise previous errors?
2. Do the new managers have experience in turning other companies around?
3. Do the managers have a convincing plan to regenerate profits and cut costs?
4. Have investors responded positively to management changes, by lifting the share price or supporting a rescue rights issue?
5. Do the debt levels seem insurmountable, requiring sales of valuable assets?
6. Have there been public rows between board members and/or advisers?
7. Does the company have strong guidance from advisers and continuing support from its banks, especially if new loans will be required?
8. Has the management agreed to keep shareholders informed as revival plans are implemented?
9. Do you have confidence that the restructured company can produce a ten-bagger result?
10. How does this recovery compare with the prospects for other companies you could invest in instead?

Ten-baggers should show strong, consistent growth. Should you be undecided about supporting a company that has become a negative ten-bagger, losing over 98 per cent of your capital? Sadly, many investors find themselves in this situation, unwilling to sell at a massive loss. I still hold 4,000 Durlacher shares, the stockbroking and corporate finance specialist. With its exposure to dotcom investments, it collapsed after the Internet bubble, from a high of 441p early in 2000 to a paltry 3p by autumn 2001. I sold the bulk of my holdings in April 2001 and made a good profit but as Durlacher is a broker I use, I hope some of its Internet investments will ultimately pay off and I wanted to retain a small stake for the long term. Investors who are undecided about a company's future might use this approach: sell enough shares at a profit or to retrieve your original stake and then hold the rest hoping for an ultimate recovery.

Investors who become active during an economic slump to stay vigilant while companies are at their most vulnerable can revert to lazy tracking when the worst of the downturn is over. Lazy trackers might also decide to be active during the first year of the portfolio's life, to remedy any early mistakes.

'Busy tracking' option

There are various measures busy trackers can undertake as situations change for their ten-bagger companies. While they will obviously do the same annual review as lazy trackers, if they have more time more options are possible.

With active tracking, the greatest benefit is being able to correct at an early date any defects that were built into the initial portfolio. As these become evident, active trackers can quickly remedy any adverse effects that prolonged exposure to such failings will inevitably bring. This gives active trackers a better chance of achieving long-term wealth targets.

The most important trap to avoid is selling holdings of future big winners before the profits arrive because a company hits what might soon prove to be merely a temporary bump on its growth path. An even worse trap is holding on to losing companies after it is obvious that they face intractable problems. Both disasters might be avoided with busy tracking routines as the guidelines listed below indicate.

Guidelines for busy trackers

1. Use the Winners' profile to spot future ten-baggers
2. Use the Losers' profile to spot potential failures at an early stage
3. Adopt a low risk portfolio by including at least seven or eight different sectors
4. Follow the focused approach favoured by hedge funds and the hedging routines used by venture capitalists
5. Spread your funds around several investments, including buying your home, saving for a pension and a FTSE All-Share Tracker; the Total Wealth Package approach
6. Carry a widely diversified portfolio of shareholdings, including a FTSE All-Share Tracker fund, to reduce the risk of large losses
7. Spend your cash in stages, paying off your mortgage and contributing to your pension and tracker funds with regular monthly payments over several years
8. Do a routine annual review of your ten-bagger portfolio to reassess the prospects for your ten candidates and modify the portfolio cautiously if or when changes seem unavoidable Regularly complete a wealth check of your total assets
9. Do not add more cash to doubtful investments
10. Sell out of failing companies in good time and reinvest the proceeds in companies showing better ten-bagger prospects

Setting stop-loss targets

Having a disciplined target helps to counter the temptation to sell and bank a small profit instead of remaining with your winning companies until they ultimately bring impressive gains. Selling decisions can be difficult, although they become easier if you have planned in advance how to deal with major problems encountered by your companies. On your initial purchase, set a stop-loss figure of 20 to 25 per cent below that buy price, intending to review the shareholding if the price falls quickly to that level. If you pay attention to the winning ten-bagger profile and buy at modest prices, this should be a rare occurrence, but it might happen as holding shares in small companies involves risk and unpredictability: they are prone to more growth hiccups than larger, better-established firms.

However, *setting* stop-loss targets helps to alert you to a falling share price to prompt a review of the company's pitfalls and attractions. But *acting* on stop-loss targets is not a feature of running a ten-bagger portfolio. A fall of 20 to 25 per cent may be an opportunity to increase your holding, although a sudden sharp drop could be warning of a stalled growth story. Avoid making hasty decisions with stop-loss prices if the general market has plunged into a prolonged downward spiral, as prices might bounce up swiftly from depressed levels with a broad revival in mood, as occurred in autumn 2001.

Look, for example, at the steep falls that hit several of my holdings during September 2001, at the height of a selling panic. I bought Amvescap shares in March 2001 at an average price of 1,044.5p, Capita Group in May at an average price of 499p and my Sage Group holding at 251p was bought in 1999. During the great autumn sell-off, all these shares fell by well over 40 per cent below my buying prices. But far from considering whether to sell I was contemplating buying more shares to hold long term.

Taking a ten-year time frame gives ample opportunity to adjust the average costs of a holding in any shares within a ten-bagger portfolio, as long as the story continues to justify confidence in the long-term promise. Over ten years you might add more funds to your growing portfolio, lifting the investment from £10,000 to £20,000 or higher, depending on how well your personal finances are growing.

The safest time to buy stocks is when people are afraid to be in the market as they were in 1974, 1982, and after the crash of 1987

Robert Prechter, founder and president of Elliott Wave International

To sell or not to sell

Of course, if you suddenly find you are holding a Marconi lookalike or a company that could follow the path taken by Baltimore Technologies or Independent Insurance, setting a stop-loss price and adhering to it as more bad news is announced could protect your wealth. But suppose you bought shares in Next and the price falls from 980p to 810p within weeks. Although this fall of 17.3 per cent looks bad, I would not be selling. If you have bought the shares to hold for ten years, the chances are that there will be a recovery in the price as Next is now a major FTSE 100 company; liquidity means it is easy to buy or sell and therefore shows great price movement volatility. A better tactic would be the one I prefer, buying my holdings in two or more blocks over a period of months. This routine also works for selling shares in companies when worrying signs appear but where you cannot decide about the long-term prospects. If you plan to sell in two stages you might find after selling half your holding that the situation stabilises, allowing you to stay invested in the company. We saw in Chapter 3 how many setbacks losing companies experience. Below is a list of warning signals that might prompt a selling decision, to avoid further losses. Compile a record from press reports of adverse events in a suspect company in your portfolio, to compare its deteriorating situation with the sell signals on this list, to help you crystallise a sell decision.

Sell signals on losing companies

1. Public boardroom conflicts that force the unexpected resignation of one or more directors
2. The announcement of a series of two or more unexpected profit warnings
3. The resignation of the company's broker, accountant, auditor or investment bank adviser with conflicts about future strategy
4. Suggestions of fraud or accounting malpractices by some directors
5. Rising debt levels possibly escalating out of control
6. Evidence of a rapid and aggressive expansion programme
7. Loss of a major client, key contract or significant order
8. Evidence that the company is not focusing on its core businesses, perhaps diversifying into different areas that may distract management
9. A poorly supported rights issue or large share sales by some directors, suggesting lack of confidence in future plans
10. Bad publicity over dealing with a crisis situation, suggesting weak management

However, if you really do want to achieve a successful ten-bagger portfolio, the chances of finding ten super growth stocks all in one intensive search are not as promising as a continuing programme of tracking which keeps you alert to new and promising situations and draws attention to other potential prospects after your initial portfolio has been set up. Reading widely in the financial press and investment magazines will keep you in touch with all the latest developments in the new issues market and new opportunities in the ever-evolving New Economy. A more active tracking programme might compensate for the low hit rate for ten-bagger success that occurs by following the automatic pilot, hands-off style of tracking or the lazy tracker route.

If you are planning for one year, plant rice.
If you are planning for ten years, plant trees.
If you are planning for a hundred years, plant people
Chinese proverb

The role of tracking

In *The Bear Book* John Rothchild discusses how investors might anticipate a new bull market as evidence shows small stocks or unit trusts investing in that sector had outperformed their big brothers in the early stages of every new bull market since 1932. Small company share prices tend to fall steeply during a decline, but, conversely, they also tend to outperform more strongly during the upturn. This small-cap advantage often lasts over several years, so anticipatory homework to ferret out small companies that could do well in the next bull market could prove profitable. Follow the financial press for information on which directors among the minnows are buying their own shares, always a positive sign. Scan websites specialising in smaller companies. The sister-site to www.mrscohen.com, www.Citywire.com, has excellent coverage. Search through *Company Refs* for tiddlers with strong profits growth, healthy revenues, good cash flow and low debts. There are bound to be some long-term winners among them. Having back-up companies you have followed for months is another way to boost returns: if you sell a losing company, you can soon replace it with a promising alternative on your reserve list.

Timely tracking is an excellent remedy for converting a mediocre portfolio into a blazing success. With very few outstanding ten-bagger companies in Britain it is even more difficult to spot them when they are young. Even adept stock pickers may find their confidence shaken by unfavourable announcements. The temptation to bank a profit can become irresistible during severe downturns, but following the discipline of the Ten-point Action

Plan might help investors escape falling prey to short-term distractions, or at least adopt a more cautious strategy. By selling half a holding or the equivalent amount to cover the initial investment, you might still enjoy the long-term promise if events reveal the growth remains intact.

We have covered the whole raft of techniques to target an outstanding portfolio performance. In Chapter 10 we bring all the themes together and will review the prospects for Vodafone as a long-term ten-bagger potential, to illustrate precisely the worries holding future ten-baggers might involve.

If you always do what you always did –
you'll always get what you always got
Anonymous

10 Get an Edge

The bottom line is that you need an edge. One of the ways you can get an edge is to find a successful system

Monroe Trout, American futures trader

The bull market of the late 1990s was certainly extraordinary. Without realising it, perhaps, we have been living through the most astonishing period of booming economies and stock markets. Through the 1990s global stock markets really did exhibit an unprecedented degree of irrational exuberance, to use the evocative phrase of Alan Greenspan, chairman of the US Federal Reserve Board. Amazing boom was rapidly followed by savage decline and for some companies – bust. Was it a false dawn? Thousands of investors were sucked into the market in the early months of 2000 near the peak, attracted by the fashionable dotcom and telecom sectors; they turned their backs on the markets during the downturn. Keeping faith in the long term is more difficult during the setbacks.

But knowing how the markets have responded to past recessions offers hope for maintaining confidence in the future. We know the markets spend more time rising than falling; they always bounce back, because they reflect the innate optimism, curiosity and creativity that is so much a part of being human.

Investors treasure hunting for ten-baggers need a new mindset for the task. To maintain a shareholding for ten years demands a high degree of perseverance grounded on confidence, which cannot emerge unless you know plenty about the companies you plan to invest in. Along the route there will be troubling moments when conditions look less than favourable, as we shall shortly discuss with Vodafone, but if you have highlighted the ten-bagger profile features that produce brilliant long-term results, you can afford to ride out the rough patches passively. To find this peace of mind does not mean you need extensive accounting knowledge or even inside information. But it does entail examining at the outset the past history, overall performance and potential of companies you plan to hold for a decade, so that you feel totally comfortable with being a long-term supporter. Peter Lynch advises against falling in love with shares in your portfolio, but a modest degree of faith based firmly on your knowledge of the company is certainly an aid to avoid falling prey to intense jitters when the smooth path to ten-bagger returns suddenly looks bumpier than you had hoped.

The market background

The pace of activity for the markets and technology is accelerating rapidly. By the time *Backing Winners* is published the performance of some of the companies featured may have changed. Readers must treat the ideas and information as a blueprint of what to do and how to do it. The chapters do not create a recipe to follow slavishly, but rather a hands-on guide of how to search for and support winning companies over the long term while rejecting losers that can deplete your wealth.

Backing Winners was mainly written during the summer and autumn of 2001, a gruelling period for equity investors as the economic outlook darkened with every passing month and in September the horrific mass murder atrocities in America escalated the uncertainties. In the UK the awesome implosion of Marconi over a matter of a few months and the abrupt collapse of Railtrack in early October, the largest corporate failure for nearly a decade, illustrated how diligent investors need to be when the economic environment turns hostile. For investors anxiously watching the values of their shares spiral down, it was a testing time, although Warren Buffett, the celebrated 'Sage of Omaha', offered a more measured perspective: 'Overall, Berkshire and its long-term shareholders benefit from a sinking stock market. When the market plummets, neither panic nor mourn.'

Freedom with m-commerce

In 2000, when Peter Keen and Ron Mackintosh wrote *The Freedom Economy** about m-commerce (commerce through mobile phones) the market for this new consumerism was minuscule, almost non-existent in volumes of global transactions. M-commerce was at the stage that e-commerce (via the Internet on a PC) had reached around 1996, when it offered a massive opportunity to grow new businesses and customer relationships but required a huge high risk investment in infrastructure and marketing. In 1996 e-commerce was in a start-up phase moving through a difficult struggle to turn promise into profitable payoff. The two authors see m-commerce as offering more promise; but greater challenges with enormous opportunities for gains or losses make it an unpredictable gamble. However, they claim m-commerce can enlarge our everyday experiences, because the wireless revolution is a technology without boundaries, a personalised province, special to every individual with a mobile phone and the enabling software for m-commerce. Each user is put uniquely at the centre of the information and communication world, instead of forcing individuals to go out and search to find the services or information they need. With m-commerce, relationships and business operations will be liberated for the benefit of the users, not the providers. In this 'freedom universe' each user sits at his own focal point, a centre, whether in his office, home, theatre or train:

*Peter Keen and Ron Mackintosh, *The Freedom Economy*, McGraw-Hill, 2001.

everything comes to the user and not the other way round. Users become masters of the m-commerce universe.

According to Peter Keen and Ron Mackintosh, 'M-commerce is the product of deregulation of telecommunications, non-regulation of the computer industry, and the Internet as largely unregulatable.' They distinguish between add-on features which are nice to have but do not change user behaviour and the trailblazing or killer applications. Hand-held devices, often called Palms, for example, are personal computers for which there are already a wide group of possible add-ons: clip-on cameras, voice mail, games, software to download music from the web, spreadsheets and word processing software visible on tiny Palm screens. These useful additions rarely change your life. Contrast this with text-messaging on digital mobile phones, which has added a new dimension to the lives of Japanese and European youngsters. At a fraction of the cost of a phone call, they can chat for hours using the shorthand language that evolved to allow text-messages to link friends and families together. Japan's DoCoMo, part of the NTT network, shows how successful this innovation has been; its profitable messaging service has 28 million regular users.

M-commerce will take time to develop and years to reach maturity but it could radically change the fundamentals of commerce and competition. This landmark development in the evolution of computing and communications has two claims to our attention. First, the conjunction of Internet and mobile phone and second, more importantly, it lies at the nub of the ever-evolving global network economy. Keen and Mackintosh think m-commerce could dominate all other e-commerce tools that now exist or emerge in the future. The technology and service quality gaps between wired and wireless appliances are shrinking remorselessly. Wireless capabilities on laptop computers and hand-helds are restricted today in speed, display qualities and functions but increasing numbers of users accept these annoying limitations because they value the freedom of mobility more.

Gradually, m-commerce will change the focus of business life and the pattern of daily affairs; first at work for corporate activities and then for people at home, at leisure, on the move, everywhere, until the customer really will be in control. This evolution goes hand in hand, literally, with the emergence of software applications, continuing utility of mobile telephony, coupled with the Internet. Mobile Internet could be the greatest enabler of the new decade and it sits at the epicentre of the expanding Network Economy but it demands a giant leap of faith to vault across the desolation of world economic prospects in the autumn of 2001 and spring of 2002 when the whole mobile telecoms sector seemed bordering on crisis. Smart investors should not lose faith: within a decade, who can say where mobile Internet will then be?

Moving mobiles

Mobile usage is exploding. MCI estimate that data traffic on the global phone system will soon overtake voice traffic, currently 1,000 times that of data but expected to flip with machines talking to machines at ten times voice traffic by 2005. Fast-access, always-on facilities will allow file transfers, data streams, photographs and charts to flash around the mobile Internet in ever-increasing volumes. The great future hope was for revolutionary third-generation mobile phone services, including unprecedented high-speed data communications and the downloading of music and video clips. On 1 October 2001 DoCoMo launched the world's first pioneering third-generation mobile phone service, where the person receiving a phone call appeared on the tiny handset screen.

Widely regarded as a huge gamble, several factors mitigated against its success. First, the more people who use the service the slower it becomes; second, serious early glitches might discourage subscribers; third, the early batteries had a short fifty-five-hour life, compared with 200 hours for DoCoMo's most advanced phones.

Forecasts of delays in handset availability for delivering the service added to the gloom. European investors fretted about 3G's technological complexities and questioned the absence of 'killer applications' which would fuel demand. Yet DoCoMo's president, Keiji Tachikawa, had enormous self-belief; he recalled that it took seven years from when they were first launched for mobile phones to become a runaway success in Japan. His enthusiasm was based on the outstanding performance achieved by DoCoMo's mobile data i-mode service with its growing army of 28 million active subscribers. He acknowledged that the investment in 3G will take time to bear fruit but remained confident of a quicker up-take than the initial launch of mobile phones in Japan. As we have seen, every pioneer is a visionary driven by the gritty determination to succeed.

Early in 2001 two of Europe's largest mobile phone networks, Telecom Italia Mobile and Vodafone, cast doubt on the so-called '2.5 generation' mobile phones due to be on the market by early 2002, although they were proving moderately successful in Japan. There were rumours of delays in introducing the high-speed Internet system, General Packet Radio Switching (GPRS), viewed as a lifeline for faster revenues by offering music downloading, games and videos on to mobiles in Europe. Second generation, WAP, Internet-enabled phones had proved a disappointment to add to delays in introducing the much-hyped third-generation services. With too many mobile contenders locked in fierce competition for subscribers, analysts thought that only five at most would survive long term.

For Vodafone shareholders, another troublesome issue was the looming technology battle with US market leader Verizon Wireless, in which Vodafone, the world's largest mobile phone operator owned a 45 per cent stake, insufficient to give it a controlling say in a dispute over which third-generation standard will be applied. Vodafone was committed to the W–CDMA (wideband – code division multiple access) version while Verizon preferred a related but incompatible CDMA 2000. Evidence shows with other appliances, such as personal computers, that before a uniform standard comes to dominate in a new technology sphere, competing standards arise which interfere with a smooth expansion of the technology itself. Over the next few years this divergence of standards might come to the fore if Verizon were to win the argument and install its preferred standard, jeopardising Vodafone's dream of genuine global roaming on a single handset.

There is no doubt in life that intensification in a niche area, with everything going into that, is how you are going to win

Sir Ernest Harrison, former chief executive of Racal Electronics

Upwardly mobile with Vodafone

When Chris Gent was knighted in the Queen's birthday honours' list of June 2001, his pleasure must have been muted by the performance of Vodafone's share price. When he was appointed chief executive in January 1997 it was 49p, but it rocketed to a high of 399p in spring 2000. That peak coincided with the outcome of the extraordinary UK auction for 3G licences to run the new broadband services of voice, data, pictures and music, and Internet for m-commerce on mobile phones. In one year the shares had lost £100 billion: investors registered their disapproval for the fast explosion in numbers of devalued shares, a paper money like any other currency, by selling Vodafone shares. At the Annual General Meeting in July 2001 shareholders from the floor protested over the breathless pace of acquisitions and the equally fast-falling share price. Lord McLaurin, Vodafone's chairman, could offer no reasonable explanation as to why the price had fallen so steeply. Many commentators, including Sir Christopher himself, insisted the spring 2000 value was totally unrealistic and was not a sensible valuation of the company at the time. In the sober light of 2001, it was clear that telecoms' over-investment and huge indebtedness within the industry were two of the major culprits causing fast-declining share values.

Chris Gent had travelled the globe buying telecoms assets in the US, Germany, Spain, Japan, New Zealand, Ireland, Mexico and Switzerland among others. In the process, he earned a reputation as a consummate dealmaker. But by mid-August 2001, when Vodafone's share price had plunged to 127p, its market capitalisation had shrunk to £86 billion. At that value the £7 billion in outstanding debt looked correspondingly more substantial, at around 8 per cent of its sinking value. Moreover, press reports noted that by October 2001, Vodafone had yet to write down the excessive prices paid for acquiring a majority stake in J-Phone, Japan's third largest mobile operator, and a small stake in China Mobile. In addition, it had yet to write off the astronomical costs of acquiring third-generation European mobile licences. While rivals BT and French-owned Orange were adjusting to the evident reality of dimming short-term 3G prospects Vodafone had £13.3 billion of licences on the balance sheet, where a figure of around £9 billion in write-offs would have seemed more cautious.

Is Vodafone overreaching itself? Can the heroic Sir Christopher Gent mastermind continued success of the company? The struggle among the telecoms titans seems remorseless. What will be the long-term outcome of this tense telecoms expansion game?

The lessons to be learned from bear markets are far more useful than those taught by bull phases. Investors who examine their mistakes are much more likely to avoid problems and maximise returns, next time around

Robert Cole, *Tempus*, *The Times*

Is Vodafone a future ten-bagger?

With all these doubts unresolved, why have I chosen to feature Vodafone as a promising ten-bagger? Yes, there are doubts, firstly about the future for mobile Internet, widely regarded in the industry as the next 'big thing' but facing a chorus of sceptical cynics. I do not see it as a one-day wonder, but investors need the patience to let the future arrive; there could be bumper profits ahead. The second serious doubt concerns the quality of management to run a successful operation of Vodafone's huge current size. As we have seen, making too many acquisitions too fast is a recipe for underperformance. Critics of Sir Christopher Gent insist he has yet to demonstrate he can run this huge enterprise with the necessary skills which are different from the skills of a consummate dealmaker. If the mobile industry is truly revolutionary, a blockbuster company operating in it can already be huge, as we saw with the formidable performance of General Electric under Jack Welch.

Before we look at Vodafone as a possible ten-bagger from its position in 2001, we should check back on the inspirational story of its parent, Racal Electronics, the electronic conglomerate run by Sir Ernest Harrison. Look at the astonishing sense of fulfilment achieved by owning shares in Racal Electronics from its float in 1961 to its finale as a public company when the last remaining part of the business was sold to Thomson–CSF, later renamed Thales, in January 2000. Like his later successor, Sir Ernest Harrison at the helm of Racal was a brilliant dealmaker, intent throughout his working life on maximising shareholder value. According to press reports at the time of the sale to Thomson–CSF, an investment of £1,000 in 1961 at Racal's flotation would have been worth £15.6 million by January 2000 when it finally ceased to exist. Over thirty-nine years, with dividends reinvested and the Vodafone shares retained, it proved to be one of the most rewarding investments on the London Stock Exchange. But it required a deep commitment plus a healthy modicum of faith. There were several share price slumps during the later years when profits did not meet expectations. So recurrent were these disappointments that they gave rise to a cynical market saying: 'Never buy ahead of a Racal results announcement.' Many investors hot on the ten-bagger trail probably lost patience with the Racal story; yet disappointing profit figures were amazingly offset by a superb thirty-nine year performance.

The road to success is always under construction

Anonymous

When I was researching the FTSE 100 top ten firms from 1988 to 1998 for *The Wealthy Investor*, only one of the ten, Glaxo, proved to be a ten-bagger, but Vodafone was climbing the lists of companies valued by market capitalisation. Launched in 1984 as a division of Racal Elecronics, it was demerged from it as Racal Telecom in 1987 at a price of 170p disregarding subsequent share splits. As we saw in Chapter 1, it had reached ten-bagger status during the 1990s, in fact by early 1998.

So let us look at Vodafone's prospects of becoming a ten-bagger company again. What is the potential for Vodafone to repeat its early performance? With numerous competitors, Vodafone is leader of the pack, with a global presence rivals cannot hope to match without future mergers in the sector; this might indeed occur. If mobile commerce (m-commerce) takes off with the launch of handsets equipped to carry broadband services, mobile operators will serve a powerful niche business with massive growth potential. It may take a decade to realise the full possibilities of the new services, but success means mobile operators who have invested heavily in 3G infrastructure will reap rich rewards. No doubt there will be failures en route, as occurs whenever pioneering innovations are being introduced, but long-term returns could reap the fruits of expansion. We must remember that taking the risk for failure has to be part of the profile for all future ten-baggers: the higher the risk, the greater the returns.

Vodafone has had a succession of visionary bosses, including Sir Ernest Harrison and Gerald Whent, whose vision for mobile telephony prompted the investment in its future development, before Sir Christopher Gent was appointed. Operating mobile services is a highly cash-generative business, although enormous debts have been incurred to buy the 3G licences and build the new networks on which the services will run. The company has been profitable in the recent past, but saw profits fall in 2000, as a result of the major acquisitions purchased to give it a global reach with nearly 96 million subscribers. Vodafone reached its target to have 100 million subscribers by financial year-end in March 2002.

For the future, if the 3G experiment works as planned, even if full implementation is delayed, there is a massive potential for growth in sales and profits. Mobile Internet and m-commerce really could be the next big things. Chris Gent has unquestionably shown his brilliant expertise as a builder of a global business but now he must exercise different skills, addressing the gigantic task of creating a blockbuster winning company, a ten-bagger share over the next decade.

Investing in any company is an act of faith in its management, its potential and the possibilities within the sector where it operates. So we can examine the features that Vodafone might have as a future ten-bagger company.

Motivation is a willingness to stop and look at things that no one else has bothered to look at

Edward de Bono, British writer and physician

Ten-bagger profile of Vodafone

Visionary chief executive with a sound business plan A series of inspired bosses have lifted Vodafone to its eminent 2001 position as one of the UK's great companies. Under Sir Christopher Gent, it was committed to remain the world's leading mobile phone operator.

Operates in a market with huge future growth potential In the late 1990s the mobile telecoms industry became one of the most exciting and revolutionary growth industries but its full potential might take years to realise.

Niche market with high entry costs to deter competitors Rapid deregulation of the mobile industry had reduced barriers to entry, but it was still difficult for other rivals to overtake Vodafone as it had created a vast global network of operations.

Opportunity to be the leading company in its sector Although Vodafone's leading position seemed fairly secure, continuous emergence of new technology and introducing 3G broadband services will be a severe test for all the operators.

Highly cash generative products and cash in the bank Mobile phone operators have repeatable and reliable cash flow. Arguably, mobiles had already become ubiquitous but essential accessories so that future revenues may be relatively immune to the slower spending that occurs during recessions. If so, mobile operators will move into the defensive sector, where revenues remain stable through recessions. Cash flows could be exponentially enhanced in due course when m-commerce allows subscribers to buy products and pay for them on their phone bills, treating mobiles like debit cards.

Low debt levels Although high costs of infrastructure development had saddled Vodafone with large debts, high recurring revenues should help to reduce them over time.

Potential to build a powerful brand Vodafone was already a globally recognised brand and it planned to rename its foreign holdings into divisions all bearing the Vodafone name, to enhance the strength of the brand still further.

Large and expanding pool of contracts, clients, markets With almost 96 million subscribers in twenty-nine countries on five continents by 2001, Vodafone had a global community and a truly global reach as the world's largest mobile phone operator.

You need courage and emotional stability to own equities and if you don't have that, maybe you shouldn't have them

John C. Bogle, founder of Vanguard Tracker Fund

Not dependent solely on one key product, market or client With the rollout of new 3G services, Vodafone's reliance on one product or market will be considerably reduced. The opportunities to prosper from broadband applications seem limitless.

Ability to evolve and develop new innovative products Although in 2001 the timing for the introduction of new services remained uncertain, given a sensible time frame, innovative and more profitable products, termed 'killer applications', most certainly will appear. As Vodafone operated one of the largest existing global networks of individuals, the possibilities for unimagined new development could be truly immense. There could possibly, in addition, be incredible cross-fertilisations within its enlarging network as this is driven by falling chip prices, expanding applications and the increasing returns of network operations.

The future looks unbelievably promising.

Ten-baggers in context

Peter Lynch introduced the exciting concept of ten-bagger winners in his book, *One Up on Wall Street.** However, as he was a renowned value investor, he adopted a cautious stance to his stock picking strategy by catering in Magellan's fund portfolio for several different categories of company, among which ten-baggers were just one. He divided his selections between stalwarts, who grow around 10 per cent a year, cyclicals who follow the fortunes of the economic cycle, recovery stocks, hoping for a revival after hitting a bad patch, and asset-plays that are sitting on something valuable, such as property, that the market is currently ignoring. Of course, he also identified growth stocks; these might be slow-growers, such as utilities that pay a generous dividend, or small aggressive fast-growers, which he described as the land of the 10–40 baggers! In a small portfolio just one or two of these could transform it, especially if the prized ten-baggers keep growing.

Every small investor should aim to follow the brilliant example set by Peter Lynch by being realistic about the risks of a concentrated portfolio. Far better to minimise those risks by spreading your funds among several different sectors and adding some slow-growers, who pay generous dividends, to create a sensible balance and tilt the odds more favourably towards long-term success.

Into the long run

Some analysts are perennial pessimists: they argue from the premise that since stocks advance on average around 10 to 11 per cent over time, the recent two decades of exceptional gains will not be repeated in the next few decades. But I think such assumptions rest on nebulous foundations. Although market patterns do tend to

*Peter Lynch, *One Up on Wall Street*, Simon & Schuster, 1989.

recur, no one can foretell how or when they will happen. But even if future returns look less exciting than in the past, this only doubles the reason for operating the Ten-point Action Plan to achieve investment success. Staying the course also eliminates the difficulty of timing the market, an illusive expertise that few consistently achieve.

Moreover, there is some evidence to imply the experts might be wrong. At present the opportunity to create a global network of networks uniting people around the world is a one-off experience whose long-term possibilities look boundless. In October 2001 the World Bank claimed that abolishing all trade barriers could boost global income by $2,800 billion (£1,954 billion), a prodigious sum, and lift 320 million people out of poverty by 2015. This is a tremendous benefit well worth striving for.

Market timing

Attempting to time the market is incredibly difficult, made nearly impossible by evidence that the best and worst weeks often follow each other closely, increasing the hazards of mistiming. The performance of the UK market following the World Trade Center outrage was a clear example: terrible losses in week 1, followed by the best ever one-week gains on the London stock market, a rise of 10.6 per cent.

Trying to guess the top of the market is equally fraught. It can tax the most experienced brains and still produce maverick results. From 1995 to 2000, numerous brokers, analysts and observers called the top of the market, only to watch it rise higher. Relying on Elliot Wave analysis, Robert Prechter forecast the Great Bear Market in 1995 in *At the Crest of the Tidal Wave**, just as the US market went into overdrive for the last five years of its Great

* Robert Prechter, *At the Crest of the Tidal Wave*, John Wiley, 1995.

Bull Run; Joe Granville had called a top in 1982, at the very moment when the Dow Jones Industrial Average began a more than fifteen-year ascent to notch up a ten-bagger rise: from 800 in 1982 the Dow reached 8,000 early in 1997. Every time the Dow hit another big round number – 2,000, 3,000, 4,000, 5,000, right up to 10,000 – someone on Wall Street was ready to call the top, as numbers of mutual funds rose, from 3,000 to 4,000 and on to an amazing 7,000. Predicting a top is as difficult as finding the low point, but investors who stay faithful to their long-term ten-bagger hopefuls and ten-year strategy need not worry about impossible short-term forecasts.

Evidence shows we should remain optimistic about long-term prospects. The three greatest bull markets of the twentieth century happened during periods of disinflation, when inflation was falling in tandem with interest rates. This combination works wonders on share prices, as was evident in 1921–9, 1949–68 and from 1982 until spring 2000. Conversely, severe bear markets coincide with either extreme inflation (rising prices) or deflation (falling prices). With the right policies periodic economic recessions or even a depression can be corrected. As noted in Chapter 1, the first half of the twentieth century was littered with recessions in America yet living standards continued to rise; while the second half of the century registered an even more sterling performance, in America, Britain and Europe.

> *A few decades from now there will be ten billion people on the planet, and sophisticated computers will be cheaper than transistor radios*
>
> David Brin, science fiction writer

An October 2001 Wealth Management supplement in the monthly magazine *Moneywise* revealed figures for the distribution of wealth in liquid assets in Britain, excluding property. There were 74,000 millionaires; 8 per cent of the UK population had assets worth between £30,000 and £200,000; nearly half of the nation's wealthy were aged forty-five to sixty-four. The global wealth management industry was worth £17 trillion, twice the size of the pensions industry. Evidence for American wealth expansion is even more impressive as during the long boom years it was increasingly tied to the stock market. Between 1983 and 1999 share ownership in America rose 86 per cent; equities as a share of financial assets rose from 19 per cent in 1989 to 38 per cent in 1999. This was an ongoing advance that had begun early in the second half of the twentieth century: in 1956 only 8.5 million Americans owned shares, one in eight of the adult population, but this had risen to one in six, or 20 million adults by the late 1960s with ever-growing numbers of investors holding stocks indirectly through company pension schemes. With the 1990s boom, the numbers of Americans holding a direct stake in the country's prosperity expanded; in 1998 40 per cent of Americans owned stock, either directly or through mutual funds and retirement accounts, up from 32 per cent in 1989. Stock ownership extended to less prosperous families; nearly one quarter of families with incomes between $10,000 and $25,000 had equity investments.

By the turn of the millennium, half of all US households owned shares directly or indirectly through mutual (collective) funds or pension plans, producing a huge pro-business constituency that will continue for at least another decade to invest in equities as the forty-year-olds save hard for retirement.

However, there is no room for complacency, with a long way to go to ensure more people can enjoy comfortable retirements. Current estimates suggest most western governments will reduce future support, and social security programmes may have been phased out by 2023.

British figures run parallel to those produced by the US Bureau of Labor Statistics Report of 1995. Out of 100 US citizens who start work at the age of twenty-five, by the age of sixty-five:

1 per cent are wealthy
3 per cent are still working
4 per cent have adequate capital for retirement
29 per cent are dead
63 per cent are dependent on social security, relatives or friends

You miss one hundred per cent of the shots you never take
Wayne Gretsky, American ice hockey player

Stay the course

The search for exciting ten-bagger candidates will never be a simple task: it requires sensible preparation and a realistic assessment of possible success. Perhaps only one, or two, or, if you are really diligent in your search and tracking skills, three companies will prove to be outstanding winners. While analysts and brokers constantly caution that the next decade will be far less profitable, investors on the lookout for remarkable companies face a tougher quest, more demanding, requiring redoubled efforts. We know the 1990s was a fantastic period for thriving companies and many appeared to be in the right sectors operating at the right time to produce brilliant results. What we need now is very much more of the same. Investors keen to find the top performers will need a strong commitment and a willingness to stay alert and vigilant over years to come. Indeed, some of my more recent company selections enjoyed fantastic growth during the millennium boom, more than meeting ten-bagger status, but I was not inclined to sell any of my winning choices during 2000, as I was firmly committed to long-term investing. A better strategy, I now realise, would have been to build up my holdings during the boom and take some part-profits as prices fell back. I have noticed that many company directors do this, selling a modest percentage of their total holdings over time.

If it's not fun, why do it?
Jerry Greenfield, co-founder of Ben & Jerry's

Get an edge

The best way to stay focused on this most exciting adventure is to get an edge that puts you ahead of the investment crowd. The secret here is very simple: regard yourself right from the outset as a part owner in the companies whose shares you purchase. This is the reason why we have followed the general histories of potential candidates stressing their strongest fundamental features rather than their financial statistical aspects, so beloved by accountants. We are not merely looking for steady, rock-solid growth, reliable dividends or low price-earnings ratios; instead we want companies with excellent products, niche markets, led by visionary chief executives determined to succeed. Just as we must stay the course to see the promise of ten-bagger potentials rewarded, so too must the directors of the companies we support.

For investors ready to focus on their long-term financial security, the prospects for improving their finances have never looked brighter. Figures from Credit Suisse First Boston, the investment bank, show that equities have outperformed cash by an annual average of 5 percentage points since 1869. In *The Bear Story* John Rothchild exposes the pitiful returns from cash against shares in the US: $100 Treasury bill bought in 1925 and rolled over for seventy years grew to $359 after deducting for inflation, while $100 invested in US shares grew into $79,187 after accounting for inflation, showing that cash cannot compete with stocks over an average lifespan.

All the evidence favours those who adopt the right attitude to investing, by following a consistent even steadfast approach.

Research by Fidelity, the fund manager, supports the view that drip-feeding money into the markets, through the good times and the bad, is an excellent way to build wealth. A notional £100 invested in the FTSE 100 every month from September 1990 – when the market was continuously falling over fears of military action in the Gulf crisis – until 3 September 2001 would have produced a fund worth £57,909, a fine return on the total of £13,200 saved over eleven years. By contrast, a nervous investor who left the market in August 1990 – when Iraq first invaded Kuwait and triggered the Gulf War – to restart a £100-a-month saving regime in January 1992 when recovery looked more evident, would have lost £3,554 to gain £54,355, illustrating the improvement that is possible by a policy of continuous investing, regardless of short-term market sentiment. American investors saw an average return of 18 per cent a year during the 1980s, but an investor who had missed the ten best days between 1982 and 1990 would have seen those returns shrink to a far more modest 5 per cent. Since 1980 $1,000 invested in shares in the Dow returned $7,000 by 2000.

By featuring Vodafone in this chapter, we can sweep the past into the present and on into a rosy future. As we saw earlier, Sir Ernest Harrison was an inspirational leader during Racal Electronic's thirty-nine years of independent life, turning £1,000 into a fortune for a faithful investor who stayed the course. Out of Racal came Vodafone, already a ten-bagger winner since 1987, and poised now on the threshold of a future promising even greater bounty.

Identifying and then keeping faith with single-minded and gifted bosses most skilled at building successful businesses is the foundation stone in the package for backing winners.

I think this is a wonderful time to be alive. There have never been so many opportunities to do things that were impossible before

Bill Gates, chairman of Microsoft

Index

H

I

J

K

L

M